my **revision** notes

OCR GCSE (9–1)

PE

Sarah Powell

my **revisi⏻n** notes

OCR GCSE (9–1)

PE

Sarah Powell

HODDER
EDUCATION
AN HACHETTE UK COMPANY

The Publishers would like to thank the following for permission to reproduce copyright material.

Photo credits: p5r spaxiax/Shutterstock.com; **p5l** Oleksii Sidorov/Shutterstock.com; **p6** Syda Productions/Shutterstock.com; **p10tr** Sebastian Kaulitzki/Shutterstock.com; **p10br** Makatserchyk/Shutterstock.com; **p11** ostill/Shutterstock.com; **p19** Andrii Muzyka/Shutterstock.com; **p21** Blamb/Shutterstock.com; **p22** wavebreakmedia/Shutterstock.com; **p30** BanksPhotos/Getty Images; **p35** Ariwasabi/Shutterstock.com; **p38** Sergei Bachlakov/Shutterstock.com; **p42** Joseph Clemson 1/Alamy Stock Photo; **p43r** Stephen Chung/Alamy Stock Photo; **p43l** Sam Stephenson/Alamy Stock Photo; **p45** Bucchi Francesco/Shutterstock.com; **p48** Kochergin/Shutterstock.com; **p49** miqu77/Shutterstock.com; **p50** Eric Fahrner/Shutterstock.com; **p55** mooinblack/Shutterstock.com; **p60** Monkey Business Images/Shutterstock.com.

Every effort has been made to trace all copyright holders, but if any have been inadvertently overlooked, the Publishers will be pleased to make the necessary arrangements at the first opportunity.

Although every effort has been made to ensure that website addresses are correct at time of going to press, Hodder Education cannot be held responsible for the content of any website mentioned in this book. It is sometimes possible to find a relocated web page by typing in the address of the home page for a website in the URL window of your browser.

Hachette UK's policy is to use papers that are natural, renewable and recyclable products and made from wood grown in well-managed forests and other controlled sources. The logging and manufacturing processes are expected to conform to the environmental regulations of the country of origin.

Orders: please contact Hachette UK Distribution, Hely Hutchinson Centre, Milton Road, Didcot, Oxfordshire, OX11 7HH. Telephone: +44 (0)1235 827827. Email education@hachette.co.uk Lines are open from 9 a.m. to 5 p.m., Monday to Friday. You can also order through our website: www.hoddereducation.co.uk

ISBN: 978 1 5104 0525 7

© 2017 Sarah Powell

First published in 2017 by
Hodder Education
An Hachette UK Company
Carmelite House, 50 Victoria Embankment
London EC4Y 0DZ

www.hoddereducation.co.uk

Impression number   12
Year   2022

Cover photo © Getty Images/iStockphoto/Thinkstock
Produced and typeset in Bembo by Gray Publishing, Tunbridge Wells, Kent
Printed in India

A catalogue record for this title is available from the British Library.

Introduction

This revision guide has been written to accompany the OCR GCSE (9–1) PE J587 specification to help you get the best possible result in your examinations. The book covers both the components that make up written exam papers 1 and 2:

- Component 01, Physical factors affecting performance, aims to examine your knowledge and understanding of the key physical factors that determine performance in physical activities and sport. The component includes:
  - the structure and function of the human body during physical activity and the physiological response to training
  - physical training using principles and developing training plans while minimising the risk of injury.
- Component 02, Socio-cultural issues and sports psychology, aims to examine your knowledge and understanding of the key socio-cultural and psychological factors that determine performance in physical activities and sport. The component includes:
  - socio-cultural influences: engagement patterns in, commercialisation of and ethical issues surrounding participation in physical activity and sport
  - sports psychology: skill, goal setting, mental preparation, guidance and feedback in physical activity and sport
  - health, fitness and well-being: health benefits of physical activity, sedentary consequences and diet and nutrition.

This book aims to give you the essentials that should serve as a reminder of what you will have covered in your course and allow you to bring together your own learning and understanding. Everyone has to decide his or her own revision strategy, but it is essential to review your work, learn it and test your understanding. These revision notes will help you to do that in a planned way, topic by topic. Use this book as the cornerstone of your revision and don't hesitate to write in it – personalise your notes and check your progress by ticking off each section as you revise.

There are a variety of activities for you to complete. There are 'now test yourself' questions at the end of every topic. Complete these and then check against the answers at the end of the book (on pages 67–74). There are also exam practice questions which aim to consolidate your revision and practise your exam skills. Also include are short revision activities.

Use the revision planner on page vi to track your progress, topic by topic. Tick each box when you have:
- revised and understood each topic
- completed the activities
- checked your answers.

You can also keep track of your revision by ticking off each topic heading in the book. You may find it helpful to add your own notes as you work through each topic.

I wish you every success with your studies.

My revision planner

Countdown to my exams

6–8 weeks to go

- Start by looking at the specification — make sure you know exactly what material you need to revise and the style of the examination. Use the revision planner on page vi to familiarise yourself with the topics.
- Organise your notes, making sure you have covered everything on the specification. The revision planner will help you to group your notes into topics.
- Work out a realistic revision plan that will allow you time for relaxation. Set aside days and times for all the subjects that you need to study, and stick to your timetable.
- Set yourself sensible targets. Break your revision down into focused sessions of around 40 minutes, divided by breaks. These Revision Notes organise the basic facts into short, memorable sections to make revising easier.

REVISED ☐

2–6 weeks to go

- Read through the relevant sections of this book and refer to the exam tips, exam summaries, typical mistakes and key terms. Tick off the topics as you feel confident about them. Highlight those topics you find difficult and look at them again in detail.
- Test your understanding of each topic by working through the 'Now test yourself' questions in the book. Look up the answers at the back of the book.
- Make a note of any problem areas as you revise, and ask your teacher to go over these in class.
- Look at past papers. They are one of the best ways to revise and practise your exam skills. Write or prepare planned answers to the exam practice questions provided in this book. Check your answers at the back of the book and try out the extra quick quizzes at **www.therevisionbutton.co.uk/myrevisionnotes**
- Use the revision activities to try out different revision methods. For example, you can make notes using mind maps, spider diagrams or flash cards.
- Track your progress using the revision planner and give yourself a reward when you have achieved your target.

REVISED ☐

One week to go

- Try to fit in at least one more timed practice of an entire past paper and seek feedback from your teacher, comparing your work closely with the mark scheme.
- Check the revision planner to make sure you haven't missed out any topics. Brush up on any areas of difficulty by talking them over with a friend or getting help from your teacher.
- Attend any revision classes put on by your teacher. Remember, he or she is an expert at preparing people for examinations.

REVISED ☐

The day before the examination

- Flick through these Revision Notes for useful reminders, for example the exam tips, exam summaries, typical mistakes and key terms.
- Check the time and place of your examination.
- Make sure you have everything you need — extra pens and pencils, tissues, a watch, bottled water, sweets.
- Allow some time to relax and have an early night to ensure you are fresh and alert for the examinations.

REVISED ☐

My exams

PE Paper 1

Date:..

Time:...

Location:...

PE Paper 2

Date:..

Time:...

Location:...

1.1 Applied anatomy and physiology

1.1a The structure and function of the skeletal system

1 Major bones and the function of the skeleton

REVISED

Location of major bones

There are many bones which make up the skeleton that shapes the framework of the body. The name and location of the major bones are shown in Figure 1.1.1.

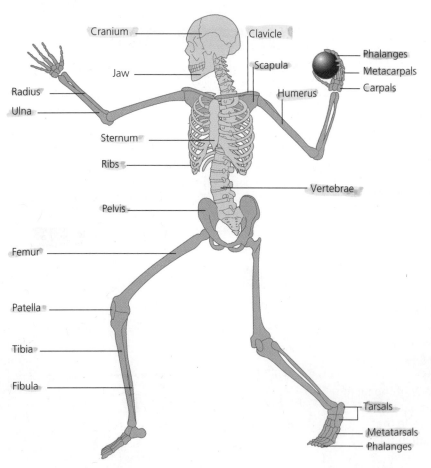

Figure 1.1.1 **Name and location of the major bones in the skeleton.**

Typical mistake

Although many bones have commonly used names, stick to the technical terminology to gain full marks. For example, cranium not skull and clavicle not collarbone.

Exam tip

It is important that you can identify the different bones on a skeleton and also identify the bones that move in the knee, elbow, shoulder and hip.

Revision activity

Group bones together and write lists of bones found in the arms, legs, head and body. In different colours highlight which bones come together to articulate at the shoulder (two bones), elbow (three bones), hip (two bones) and knee (two bones).

Functions of the skeleton

The skeleton has five main functions:
- It provides a shaping framework which gives the body **support** and **posture**. For example, the vertebrae support the weight of the upper body and hold the body upright to keep good posture.
- It gives **protection** to keep the internal organs from damage or injury. For example, the cranium protects a footballer's brain when heading a ball.
- It allows **movement** by providing areas for muscles to attach and form lever systems. For example, the biceps attaches to the upper and lower arm, creating movement at the elbow.
- Some large bones contain marrow which produces **blood cells**. For example, red blood cells are produced to transport oxygen around the body.
- It stores **minerals**, such as calcium, potassium and iron, and slowly releases them into the blood. For example, calcium is essential to move our muscles and keep our bones healthy.

Now test yourself

TESTED

1 Which two bones are found in the lower leg?
2 Which two bones are found in the forearm?
3 Which set of bones run the length of the back?
4 Which bone protects the brain?
5 Which bones protect the heart and lungs?
6 The muscles attach to the bones to create what?
7 True or false? Two functions of the skeleton are to produce blood cells and to store minerals.

> **Exam tip**
>
> Make sure you can identify the five functions of the skeleton and also apply these functions to examples.

2 Synovial joints, ligaments, tendons and cartilage

REVISED

Synovial joints

Synovial joints are freely movable joints where two or more bones articulate (see Figure 1.1.2). They allow for the wide range of movements that are essential when participating in sport. They have a joint capsule to strengthen the joint and synovial fluid to allow friction-free movement.

> **Synovial joint** A freely movable joint where two or more bones articulate

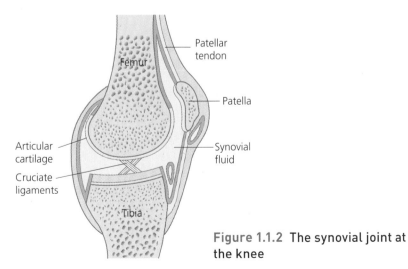

Figure 1.1.2 The synovial joint at the knee

> **Exam tip**
>
> Although the individual synovial joints, such as the knee and shoulder, may look different they will share the same common features.

Ligaments, tendons and cartilage

Ligaments, tendons and cartilage are also important components of joints:

- **Ligaments** connect bone to bone. They are strong bands of connective tissue which join bones together, keep joints stable and prevent extreme movements which could lead to dislocation. An example of a group of ligaments is the cruciate ligaments which connect the femur and tibia in the knee joint.
- **Tendons** connect muscle to bone. They are tough bands of connective tissue which transmit forces generated by the muscles to move bones into position. An example of a tendon is the Achilles tendon which connects the gastrocnemius to the heel bone.
- Cartilage reduces friction and absorbs shock to protect a joint. It is a tough and flexible connective tissue which exists in two forms:
  - ○ **articular cartilage** covers the articulating surfaces of bones; it protects the bone by reducing friction
  - ○ white fibrocartilage is found in areas of great stress, such as the knee (meniscus) or spine (vertebral discs); it protects the bones by absorbing shock and allows the bones to fit together smoothly.

The hinge joint and ball and socket joint are two types of synovial joints essential to sport.

Hinge joint

A hinge joint allows movement in one plane. There are two hinge joints in the human body:

- **Elbow**: the humerus, radius and ulna articulate to perform movement such as touching your shoulder, throwing a dart or a biceps curl.
- **Knee**: the femur and tibia articulate to perform movement such as squatting down or kicking a ball.

> **Ligament** Tissue which connects bone to bone and stabilises joints
>
> **Tendon** Tissue which connects muscle to bone and transmits muscular forces to move bones
>
> **Articular cartilage** Tissue which covers the surface of articulating bones to prevent friction, absorb shock and protect bone surface

> **Typical mistake**
>
> There are only two bones which articulate within the knee joint: the femur and tibia. The patella and fibula do not articulate in the knee joint.

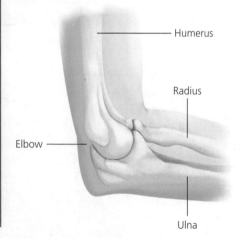

Figure 1.1.3 The elbow joint enables the arm to bend and straighten.

Ball and socket joint

A ball and socket joint allows a wide range of motion in all three planes:

● **Shoulder**: the scapula and humerus articulate to perform movement such as throwing a javelin or serving in tennis.
● **Hip**: the pelvis and femur articulate to perform movement such as sit–ups or the splits.

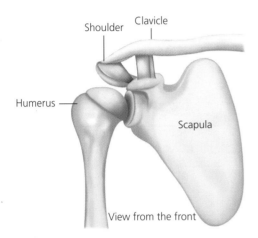

Figure 1.1.4 The shoulder joint allows us to swing our arms and to move them outwards and inwards.

Now test yourself

TESTED ☐

1 Identify the key word from the following statements:
   a) connective tissue which connects bone to bone
   b) a freely movable joint where two or more bones articulate
   c) a type of joint which restricts movement to only one plane.
2 What is the function of articular cartilage?
3 Name an example of a tendon.
4 Which bones articulate in the elbow joint?
5 Which bones articulate in the hip joint?
6 True or false? The articulating bones of the knee joint are the femur, tibia and fibula.
7 True or false? White fibrocartilage absorbs shock and helps the vertebrae to fit smoothly together.

3 Movement at hinge and ball and socket joints

Movements at hinge joints

Hinge joints allow movement in one plane:

- **flexion**: a decrease in joint angle
- **extension**: an increase in joint angle.

Table 1.1.1 Hinge joint movements in sport

Joint	Flexion	Extension
Elbow	Upward (lifting) phase of a biceps curl	Downward (lowering) phase of a biceps curl
Knee	Downward (lowering) phase of a squat	Upward (lifting) phase of a squat

Figure 1.1.5 Hinge joint movement: elbow flexion.

Figure 1.1.6 Hinge joint movement: knee extension.

Movements at ball and socket joints

Ball and socket joints at the shoulder and hip allow movement in three planes:

- **flexion**: a decrease in joint angle (to the front of the body)
- **extension**: an increase in joint angle (to the back of the body)
- **abduction**: movement away from the body (out to the side)
- **adduction**: movement towards the body (in to the middle)
- **rotation**: movement around a limb's long axis (screwdriver action)
- **circumduction**: a combination of movements allowing a continuous circular movement of a limb (arm circles).

> **Revision activity**
>
> Look at the sports pages of a magazine or a newspaper. Analyse as many athletes as you can, identifying the movements at the elbow, knee, shoulder and hip joints.

> **Revision activity**
>
> Redraw and complete a table for each joint including a column for joint type, articulating bones and movement patterns.

Table 1.1.2 Ball and socket movements in sport

Joint	Flexion	Extension	Abduction	Adduction	Rotation	Circumduction
Shoulder	Execution phase of an underarm throw	Preparation phase (backswing) of an underarm throw	Outward phase of a star jump	Inward phase of a star jump	Placing spin on a tennis ball in a forehand groundstroke	Arm circles in a warm-up
Hip	Execution phase of a rugby conversion kick	Preparation phase of a rugby conversion kick	Outward phase of a star jump	Inward phase of a star jump	Ballet dancer moving into first position	Movement of the trail leg up and over a hurdle

Figure 1.1.7 Ball and socket movement: hip abduction.

Now test yourself

1 Give a sporting example of the following movements:
   a) flexion of the elbow
   b) extension of the knee
   c) abduction of the shoulder
   d) rotation of the hip.
2 Which movement would you associate with the following statements?
   a) an increase in joint angle
   b) movement around a limb's long axis (a screwdriver action)
   c) movement towards the middle of the body
   d) a combination of movements allowing a continuous circular action.
3 True or false? A hinge joint only has one plane of movement whereas a ball and socket has three.
4 True or false? Circumduction is a movement pattern associated with hinge joints only.
5 True or false? The movement of the legs to the side of the body away from the midline is known as adduction.

Figure 1.1.8 Ball and socket movement: shoulder circumduction.

Exam practice

1 The articulating bones in the knee joint are:
   a) femur, tibia and fibula
   b) femur, fibula and patella
   c) femur and tibia
   d) femur, tibia, fibula and patella. [1]
2 The articulating bones in the shoulder joint are:
   a) humerus and scapula
   b) humerus, scapula and clavicle
   c) humerus, scapula and sternum
   d) humerus, radius and ulna. [1]
3. The movements possible at a ball and socket joint are:
   a) abduction and adduction
   b) flexion and extension
   c) rotation and circumduction
   d) all of the above. [1]
4 Identify and describe two functions of the skeleton. [2]
5 Define a synovial joint and identify the type of joint found at the shoulder and at the knee. [2]
6 Using your anatomical knowledge complete the following table: [6]

Joint	Type of joint	Articulating bones	Movement	Sorting example
Elbow			Flexion	
Hip				Upward phase of a squat

Summary

- The skeleton's main functions are to provide a shaping framework for support and posture, protect internal organs from damage, provide areas for muscle to attach to allow movement, and produce blood cells and store minerals.
- A synovial joint is a freely movable joint where two or more bones articulate.
- Ligaments connect bone to bone and keep joints stable, for example cruciate ligaments.
- Tendons connect muscle to bone and transmit muscular force to move bones, for example the Achilles tendon.
- Articular cartilage protects the bone surface at joints by reducing friction and absorbing shock.
- Hinge joints allow movement patterns of flexion and extension:
  - elbow: humerus, radius and ulna articulate
  - knee: femur and tibia articulate.

- Ball and socket joints allow movement patterns of flexion, extension, abduction, adduction, rotation and circumduction:
  - shoulder: scapula and humerus articulate
  - hip: pelvis and femur articulate
- Application of joint movement examples;
  - elbow flexion: preparation of a free throw shot in basketball where the elbow flexes to bring the ball closer to the shoulder
  - knee extension: execution phase of a high jump where the knee extends to straighten the leg at take-off
  - shoulder abduction: outward phase of a star jump as the shoulder joint moves the arm out to the side
  - hip rotation: a ballet dancer rotates their hip outwards as they move into first position.

Quick quizzes at **www.hoddereducation.co.uk/myrevisionnotes**

1.1b The structure and function of the muscular system

4 Major muscle groups and the roles that they play

REVISED

Location of the major muscle groups

Muscles attach to the skeleton and use forces to create movement. The names and locations of the major muscle groups are shown in Figure 1.1.9.

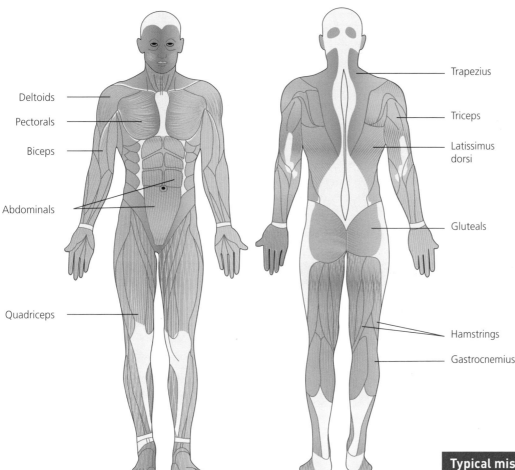

Deltoids

Pectorals

Biceps

Abdominals

Quadriceps

Trapezius

Triceps

Latissimus dorsi

Gluteals

Hamstrings

Gastrocnemius

Figure 1.1.9 Name and location of the major muscle groups in the body.

Muscles create movement. They generate a force by contracting which transfers to the bones by tendons. This creates a lever system to move the bones into different positions. Tables 1.1.3 and 1.1.4 (page 10) show the major muscle groups by the joints they move and movement patterns, accompanied by specific sporting examples.

Typical mistake

Although many muscle groups have commonly used names, stick to the technical terminology to gain full marks, for example: abdominals not abs and pectorals not pecs.

Exam tip

It is important you can identify the different muscle groups in a diagram and also identify the muscle group that works to move a specific joint.

Revision activity

Pair up muscle groups with the joints that they move and apply to a sport of your choice.

Table 1.1.3 Muscle groups, movement patterns and sporting examples of the elbow and shoulder

Joint	Muscle group	Movement	Example
Elbow	Biceps	Flexion	The biceps flexes the elbow in the upward phase of a biceps curl
	Triceps	Extension	The triceps extends the elbow to shoot the ball in netball
Shoulder	Deltoids	Flexion Extension Abduction	The deltoids: • flex the shoulder of a tennis player as they throw the ball up to serve • extend the shoulder joint of a rounders player as they draw the arm back to bowl the ball • abduct the shoulder joint in the outward phase of a star jump
	Latissimus dorsi	Adduction	The latissimus dorsi adducts the shoulder in the inward phase of a star jump
	Pectorals	Adduction in a horizontal plane (arm moves across the chest)	The pectorals horizontally adduct the arm across the chest during the release of a discus
	Trapezius	Abduction of the shoulder in a horizontal plane (arm moves out from the chest)	The trapezius horizontally abducts the shoulder to bring the arm back in the preparation phase of the discus

Table 1.1.4 Muscle groups, movement patterns and sporting examples of the knee, vertebral column, hip and ankle

Joint	Muscle group	Movement	Example
Knee	Quadriceps	Extension	The quadriceps extend the knee during the execution phase of kicking a football
	Hamstrings	Flexion	The hamstrings flex the knee in the preparation phase of kicking a football
Vertebral column	Abdominals	Flexion (bending forwards)	The abdominals flex the vertebral column and hip joint in the upward phase of a sit-up
Hip	Gluteals	Extension Abduction Rotation	The gluteals: • extend the hip as a ballet dancer performs an arabesque • abduct the hip in the outward phase of a star jump • rotate the hip as a ballet dancer moves into first position
Ankle	Gastrocnemius	Plantar flexion (pointing the toes)	The gastrocnemius plantar flexes a ballet dancer's ankle as they go *en pointe*

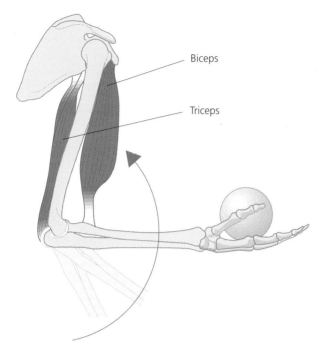

Figure 1.1.10 The biceps creates flexion of the elbow.

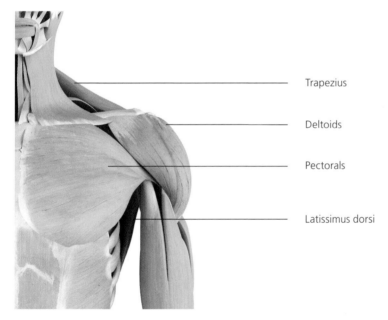

Figure 1.1.11 The major muscle groups around the shoulder joint.

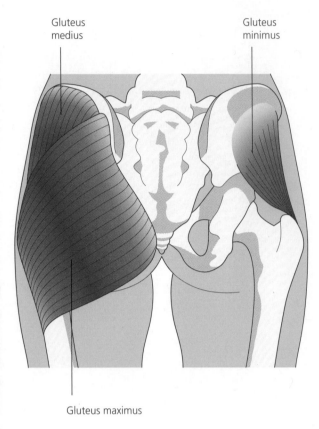

Gluteus medius

Gluteus minimus

Gluteus maximus

Figure 1.1.12 The gluteal muscle group around the hip joint.

Gastrocnemius

Plantar flexion of the ankle joint

Figure 1.1.13 Plantar flexion of the ankle joint by the gastrocnemius during a calf raise exercise.

The roles of muscles in movement

Muscles never work alone. They work in pairs or groups to create co-ordinated movement. Each muscle contracts to shorten, lengthen or stay the same length while producing a force.

There are three main roles a muscle can act in:
- **agonist**: a muscle which creates movement (the working muscle or prime mover)
- **antagonist**: a muscle which co-ordinates and controls movement (opposes the agonist to provide a breaking force)
- **fixator**: a muscle which stabilises one part of the body while another one moves.

When performing the upward phase of the biceps curl:
- the agonist is the biceps creating flexion at the elbow
- the antagonist is the triceps which co-ordinates the action
- the fixators are the shoulder muscles which keep the scapula in place.

Antagonistic muscle action is the co-ordinating action of an agonist and antagonist working together. As one muscle creates the movement (for example flexion) its antagonistic pair will co-ordinate the action. During the opposite movement (for example extension) the two muscles will swap roles. Here is an example:
- When kicking a football, in the preparation phase the hamstrings act as the agonist to create flexion of the knee as the quadriceps act as the antagonist to co-ordinate the action.
- In the execution phase, the quadriceps become the agonist to create extension of the knee and the hamstrings become the antagonist to co-ordinate the action.

> **Agonist** A muscle which creates movement
>
> **Antagonist** A muscle which co-ordinates movement
>
> **Fixator** A muscle which stabilises one part of the body during movement

Quadriceps acting as the antagonist to co-ordinate flexion of the knee joint

Quadriceps acting as the agonist to create extension of the knee joint

Figure 1.1.14 The role of the quadriceps as both an agonist and antagonist muscle group.

Revision activity

Create a table of antagonistic pairs: muscles or groups of muscles that work together. You could extend this table to include the movements they produce when they act as the agonist, as shown below:

Joint	Antagonistic pair (movement created)	
Elbow	Biceps (flexion)	Triceps (extension)
Knee	Hamstrings (flexion)	Quadriceps (extension)

Now test yourself

TESTED ☐

1. Which two muscles are found in the upper arm near the humerus?
2. Which muscle is found in the lower leg behind the tibia?
3. Which movement is created by the abdominals?
4. Which movement is created by the latissimus dorsi?
5. What is the antagonistic pair to the quadriceps?
6. True or false? An agonist stabilises an area of the body as another part moves.
7. True or false? Antagonistic pairs work together to co-ordinate movement.
8. True or false? The gastrocnemius and gluteals are antagonistic pairs.

Exam practice

1 The agonist for hip rotation is the:
  a) quadriceps
  b) gluteals
  c) abdominals
  d) gastrocnemius. [1]
2 The agonist for shoulder adduction is the:
  a) pectorals
  b) deltoids
  c) latissimus dorsi
  d) abdominals. [1]
3 The role of a muscle when acting as a fixator is:
  a) to co-ordinate movement
  b) to stabilise one area of the body during movement
  c) to create movement
  d) to work with an opposing muscle group. [1]
4 Define the term agonist and give an example from a sport of your choice. [2]
5 Using a sporting example, describe the function of an antagonistic pair. [2]
6 Using your anatomical knowledge, complete the following table: [4]

Joint	Type of joint	Movement	Agonist	Antagonist
Shoulder	Ball and socket	Abduction		
Knee	Hinge		Quadriceps	

Summary

- Muscles create movement by producing a force which during contraction pulls on the bones.
- Muscles or muscle groups are responsible for specific joint movements, for example:
  - biceps – elbow flexion
  - triceps – elbow extension
  - deltoids – shoulder flexion, extension and abduction
  - latissimus dorsi – shoulder adduction.
- Muscles can act in three main roles:
  - as an agonist a muscle creates the movement
  - as an antagonist a muscle co-ordinates the action
  - as a fixator a muscle stabilises part of the body while another part moves.
- Muscles act as antagonistic pairs to create a co-ordinated action. As one muscle acts as the agonist to create the movement, its antagonistic pair acts as the antagonist to co-ordinate the action.

1.1c Movement analysis

5 Lever systems

Components of a lever system

A lever system is the co-ordination of bones and muscles to create movement. Lever systems have four component parts:

- **lever**: a bone
- **fulcrum**: a joint
- **effort**: muscular force
- **load**: weight of a body part or object.

For example, in the upward phase of a biceps curl, the biceps is attached to the radius bone (lever) and generates muscular force (effort) to pull the radius upwards at the elbow joint (fulcrum). The larger the weight being lifted (load), the greater the muscular force needs to be.

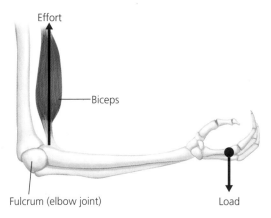

Figure 1.1.15 The lever system at the elbow during the upward phase of a biceps curl.

Types of lever system

There are three types of lever system based on the order of the fulcrum, effort and load. They can be drawn with a simple diagram as shown in Table 1.1.5.

Table 1.1.5 Classification of lever system with sporting examples

Class of lever	Order of components	Diagram	Sporting example
First class	Effort – fulcrum – load	Effort — Fulcrum — Load	Extension of the neck as a footballer prepares to head a football Extension of the elbow in an overarm throw in cricket
Second class	Fulcrum – load – effort	Fulcrum — Load — Effort	Plantar flexion of the ankle as a basketballer uses the ball of the foot to take off for a jump shot
Third class	Fulcrum – effort – load	Fulcrum — Effort — Load	Flexion of the elbow during the upward phase of a biceps curl Extension of the knee as a footballer executes a pass

The most efficient is a second class lever system as it has the **mechanical advantage**. This is the ability to move a large load with a small effort due to the effort being further from the fulcrum than the load.

> **Mechanical advantage**
> The ability of a lever system to move a large load with a small effort

> **Exam tip**
>
> Come up with a rhyme to help you remember the component order of each lever system. Only the middle component is important, such as 1, 2, 3 think F, L, E.

1 What acts as a lever?
2 What acts as a fulcrum?
3 What is the component order of a third class lever system?
4 Give a sporting example of the use of a first class lever system.
5 True or false? A first class lever system will always have the effort in the middle between the load and fulcrum.
6 True or false? The mechanical advantage is the ability for a lever system to move a limb at great speed.
7 Fill in the blanks. A high jumper will take off and jump upwards towards the bar. The lever system at the ball of the foot is an example of a _____ class lever system. The fulcrum is the joint at the ball of the foot, the effort is the _____ _____ generated by the gastrocnemius and the load is the _____ of the high jumper.

6 Planes of movement and axes of rotation

REVISED

Planes of movement

We describe movement in three dimensions, based on the three **planes of movement**: sagittal, frontal and transverse.

> **Plane of movement** Three-dimensional movements at a joint

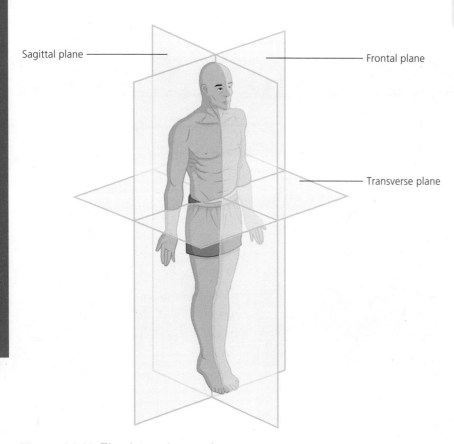

Sagittal plane

Frontal plane

Transverse plane

Figure 1.1.16 The three planes of movement.

Table 1.1.6 Planes of movement and sporting examples

Plane	Description	Movements	Sporting example
Sagittal	A plane of movement which vertically splits the body into left and right parts	Flexion Extension	Shoulder, hip and knee flexion during the running action
Frontal	A plane of movement which vertically splits the body into front and back parts	Abduction Adduction	Shoulder and hip abduction in the outward phase of a star jump
Transverse	A plane of movement which horizontally splits the body into upper and lower parts	Rotation	Shoulder rotation as a tennis player puts spin on the ball

Axes of rotation

A body can move around three **axes of rotation**: longitudinal, frontal and transverse.

Table 1.1.7 Axes of rotation and sporting examples

Axis	Description	Sporting example
Longitudinal	A vertical axis which runs from the top to the bottom of the body	An ice skater performing a flat spin
Frontal	A horizontal axis running from the front to the back of the body	A gymnast performing a cartwheel
Transverse	A horizontal axis running from side to side	A high-board diver performing a somersault

> **Axis of rotation**
> An imaginary line about which a body can rotate

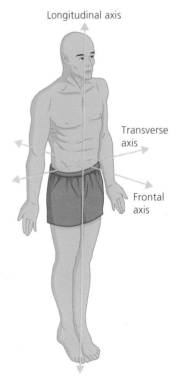

Longitudinal axis

Transverse axis

Frontal axis

Figure 1.1.17 The three axes of rotation.

Now test yourself

TESTED ☐

1 Identify the plane of movement for the following actions:
   a) flexion of the elbow
   b) abduction of the hip
   c) rotation of the shoulder.
2 Give a sporting example of movement along the transverse plane.
3 How does the longitudinal axis of rotation pass through the body?
4 True or false? A goalkeeper diving to the top right-hand corner of the goal rotates around the transverse axis.
5 True or false? The rotation of a discus thrower in the wind-up phase is an example of rotation around the longitudinal axis.

> **Revision activity**
> Try to identify as many sporting situations as possible where the body rotates around one or more of the axes of rotation.

Exam practice

1 The component order of a first class lever is:
   a) fulcrum – load – effort
   b) effort – load – fulcrum
   c) load – effort – fulcrum
   d) load – fulcrum – effort. [1]

2 A cartwheel occurs around which axis of rotation?
   a) transverse
   b) sagittal
   c) frontal
   d) longitudinal. [1]

3 Which of these is an example of movement along the transverse plane?
   a) hip abduction
   b) hip rotation
   c) hip flexion
   d) hip extension. [1]

4 Define the term mechanical advantage and state which class of lever it is most associated with. [2]

5 Using a sporting example, analyse the use of a third class lever in the human body. [4]

Summary

- A lever system comprises a lever, fulcrum, effort and load. There are three classes of lever depending on the order of their component parts:
  - first class lever: load – fulcrum – effort
  - second class lever: fulcrum – load – effort
  - third class lever: fulcrum – effort – load.
- Second class levers have the mechanical advantage to move a large load with a relatively small effort as the effort is furthest from the fulcrum.
- Sagittal plane of movement vertically splits the body into left and right parts, for example flexion and extension.
- Frontal plane of movement vertically splits the body into front and back parts, for example abduction and adduction.
- Transverse plane of movement horizontally splits the body into upper and lower parts, for example rotation.
- Longitudinal axis of rotation runs vertically from the top to the bottom of the body, for example a pirouette in dance.
- Frontal axis of rotation runs horizontally from the front to the back of the body, for example a cartwheel in gymnastics.
- Transverse axis of rotation runs horizontally from side to side of the body, for example a somersault in trampolining.

1.1d The cardiovascular and respiratory system

7 Cardiovascular system

REVISED

Double circulatory system

Blood is contained within the circulatory system. It flows continuously through the heart and around the systemic and pulmonary circuits:

- **Systemic circuit**: transports **oxygenated blood** from the heart around the body and **deoxygenated blood** back to the heart. The systemic circuit delivers oxygen and nutrients to the muscles during exercise and removes waste products.
- **Pulmonary circuit**: transports deoxygenated blood from the heart around the lungs and oxygenated blood back to the heart. The pulmonary circuit removes carbon dioxide from the bloodstream and replenishes oxygen stores.

Blood vessels

The vascular system consists of three types of blood vessels: **arteries**, **capillaries** and **veins**. Their structure and function are summarised in Table 1.1.8.

Table 1.1.8 Structure and function of the three blood vessel types

Blood vessels	Structure	Function
Arteries: the main artery is the aorta which divides into smaller arteries and further into arterioles	Smooth muscle layer which vasodilates (widens) and vasoconstricts (narrows) to control blood flow	Carry oxygenated blood at high pressure from the heart to the muscles and organs to deliver oxygen and nutrients to the tissues
Capillaries	Single-cell-thick wall to allow for gaseous exchange	Gaseous exchange through a dense network of capillaries around muscles and alveoli
Veins: venules connect to form smaller veins and further to form the main vein, the vena cava	Thin layer of smooth muscle and pocket valves to prevent the backflow of blood	Carry deoxygenated blood at low pressure back to the heart against gravity

Oxygenated blood Blood rich in oxygen and nutrients

Deoxygenated blood Blood rich in carbon dioxide and waste products

Artery A blood vessel which transports oxygenated blood from the heart to the muscles and organs

Capillary Thin-walled blood vessel which brings blood in close contact with muscles and organs for gaseous exchange

Vein A blood vessel which transports deoxygenated blood from the body to the heart

Revision activity

Draw a diagram of the double circulatory system connecting the heart with the systemic and pulmonary circuits of blood flow.

The path of blood through the heart

The heart functions as a double pump where the two sides, positioned side by side, have atria at the top and ventricles at the bottom:

- the left side has a thick muscular wall to pump oxygenated blood to the muscles and organs with more force
- the right side pumps deoxygenated blood to the lungs to remove carbon dioxide.

The septum separates the left and right sides to prevent oxygenated and deoxygenated blood mixing. Bicuspid, tricuspid and semi-lunar valves prevent the backflow of blood through the heart.

The major blood vessels exiting the heart are:

- **aorta**: carries oxygenated blood from the left ventricle to the muscles and organs
- **vena cava**: carries deoxygenated blood from the muscles and organs to the right atrium
- **pulmonary artery**: carries deoxygenated blood from the right ventricle to the lungs
- **pulmonary vein**: carries oxygenated blood from the lungs to the left atrium.

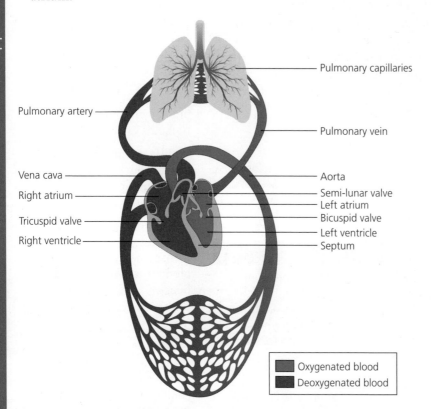

Figure 1.1.18 A simplified plan of the cardiovascular system.

Labels: Pulmonary capillaries, Pulmonary artery, Pulmonary vein, Vena cava, Aorta, Right atrium, Semi-lunar valve, Left atrium, Tricuspid valve, Bicuspid valve, Right ventricle, Left ventricle, Septum

Legend: Oxygenated blood / Deoxygenated blood

Heart rate, stroke volume and cardiac output

Heart rate (HR) is the number of heart contractions each minute, measured in beats per minute (bpm). At rest, the average HR is around 72 bpm, but it can rise up to 200 bpm in intense exercise.

Stroke volume (SV) is the volume of blood ejected from the left ventricle each beat, measured in millilitres (ml).

Cardiac output (Q) is the volume of blood ejected from the left ventricle each minute, measured in litres per minute (l/min).

Cardiac output (Q) = heart rate (HR) × stroke volume (SV).

Heart rate (HR) The number of heart contractions each minute (bpm)

Stroke volume (SV) The volume of blood ejected from the left ventricle each beat (ml)

Cardiac output (Q) The volume of blood ejected from the left ventricle each minute (l/min)

Red blood cells

Blood consists of red and white cells surrounded by fluid called plasma. White cells (leucocytes) serve to fight infection. The plasma contains nutrients essential for energy production.

Red blood cells (erythrocytes) contain **haemoglobin** which carries oxygen in the bloodstream. Aerobic training increases the volume of red blood cells in the bloodstream. The greater the volume of red blood cells, the greater the efficiency of oxygen transport and aerobic energy production.

Haemoglobin An iron-rich protein found in red blood cells which transports oxygen in the bloodstream

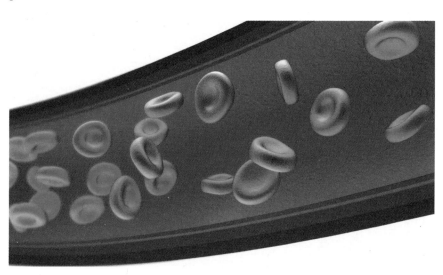

Figure 1.1.19 A representation of red blood cells flowing through an artery.

Now test yourself

TESTED ☐

1 Where does the pulmonary circuit go from and to?
2 Which blood vessel has a thick layer of smooth muscle?
3 Which blood vessel has very thin walls?
4 Fill in the following gaps to describe the systemic flow of blood through the heart. The _____ carries oxygenated blood from the left _____ to the muscles and organs. Oxygen moves through the _____ walls into the tissues and carbon dioxide is collected. The _____ carries this deoxygenated blood back to the right _____.
   (Word bank: atrium / aorta / vena cava / capillary / ventricle.)
5 True or false? The pulmonary vein carries oxygenated blood back to the heart from the lungs.
6 True or false? Heart rate is measured in millilitres (ml).
7 True or false? Cardiac output can be measured by multiplying heart rate by stroke volume.
8 What carries oxygen in the bloodstream?

8 Respiratory system

Pathway of air

Air is drawn into the respiratory system through the nose and mouth, which warm, moisten and filter the air. It passes down the trachea which divides into two bronchi feeding the left and right lungs. The bronchi branch into bronchioles, spreading the air out through the lung tissue to reach the alveoli, where gaseous exchange takes place.

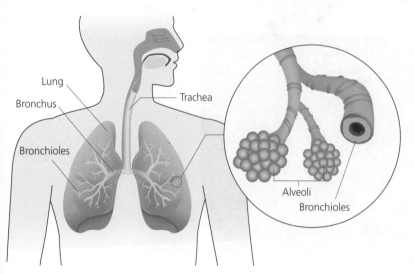

Figure 1.1.20 **The key features of the respiratory system.**

Alveoli

Gaseous exchange between the lungs and the bloodstream takes place at the **alveoli**. The alveoli are composed of a single-cell-thick wall with a moist lining and are covered in capillaries. They are the site where carbon dioxide from deoxygenated blood is exchanged for oxygen in order to fill the red blood cells.

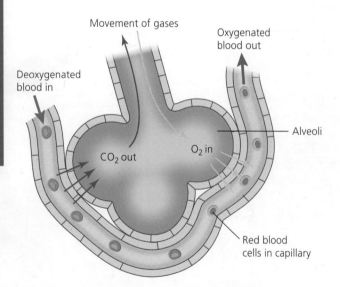

Figure 1.1.21 **Gaseous exchange at the alveoli.**

> **Exam tip**
>
> Make sure you are able to describe and also label a diagram to show the pathway of air through the respiratory system.

> **Gaseous exchange**
> The movement of oxygen and carbon dioxide between the alveoli and bloodstream
>
> **Alveoli** Clusters of tiny air sacs covered in capillaries which allow gaseous exchange

Quick quizzes at **www.hoddereducation.co.uk/myrevisionnotes**

All gases move from an area of high concentration to an area of low concentration, therefore:

- carbon dioxide (CO_2), which is in a high concentration in deoxygenated blood arriving at the alveoli, **diffuses** into the alveoli to be expired
- oxygen (O_2), which is in a high concentration in the alveoli, diffuses into the bloodstream to be collected by the red blood cells.

Role of respiratory muscles

There are two key muscles responsible for breathing in (inspiration) and breathing out (expiration) at rest: the **diaphragm** and **intercostals**. When these muscles contract, the effect is to draw air into the lungs (see Table 1.1.9).

Table 1.1.9 The structure, function and effect of respiratory muscle contraction to create inspiration

Structure	Function	Effect
Diaphragm flattens underneath the rib cage Intercostals pull on the ribs to lift the rib cage up and out	Increase the volume of the chest cavity which decreases the pressure inside the lungs	Air is drawn into the lungs (inspiration)

When the diaphragm and intercostals relax, the rib cage moves in and down, which decreases the chest cavity volume, which in turn raises the pressure, pushing air out of the lungs (expiration).

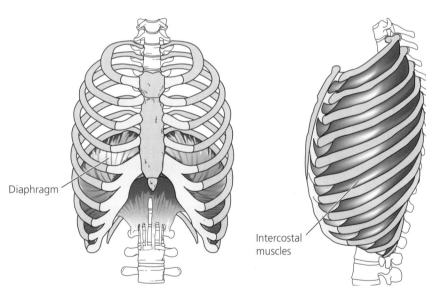

Figure 1.1.22 The respiratory muscles.

Breathing rate, tidal volume and minute ventilation

Breathing rate (f) is the number of inspirations or expirations taken each minute (breaths per minute). At rest, the average breathing rate is 12–15 breaths every minute. **Tidal volume (TV)** is the volume of air inspired or expired in one breath, measured in millilitres (ml). **Minute ventilation (VE)** is the volume of air inspired or expired each minute, measured in litres per minute (l/min).

> Minute ventilation (VE) = breathing frequency (f) × tidal volume (TV).

Diffusion Movement of gases across a membrane from an area of high to low concentration

Breathing frequency (f) The number of inspirations or expirations each minute (breaths/min)

Tidal volume (TV) The volume of air inspired or expired each breath (ml)

Minute ventilation (VE) The volume of air inspired or expired each minute (l/min)

Typical mistake

Carbon dioxide moves **out** of the blood into the alveoli to be expired and oxygen moves **into** the bloodstream from the air inspired. Make sure you get them the right way round!

Revision activity

Create a table or flowchart using these four titles: muscles, movement, volume, pressure. Describe which muscles create what movement, how it affects volume and how this affects pressure. Follow this procedure once for inspiration and once for expiration.

Exam tip

HR, SV and Q are very similar in definition, units and calculation to f, TV and VE.

Now test yourself   TESTED ☐

1 Identify the key word from the following statements:
   a) clusters of tiny air sacs which allow for gaseous exchange
   b) the movement of gases across a membrane from an area of high to low concentration
   c) the number of inspirations or expirations taken per minute.
2 How do you calculate minute ventilation?
3 What is an average resting breathing rate?
4 What do the diaphragm and intercostals do to lead to breathing out (an expiration)?
5 Describe the pathway of air from the nose to the alveoli.

9 Aerobic and anaerobic exercise

REVISED ☐

Aerobic versus anaerobic exercise

Specific sports or exercises can be aerobic or anaerobic in nature, or even a combination of both depending on the intensity and duration of activity.

Table 1.1.10 Aerobic versus anaerobic exercise

	Aerobic	Anaerobic
Description	Activity that raises heart and breathing rate which can be sustained over time	Activity that pushes the performer to maximum and can lead to the performer being out of breath and fatigued
Energy production	With oxygen	Without oxygen
Intensity	Low to moderate	High
Duration	Long	Short
Example	Jogging	Sprinting
By-products	Carbon dioxide and water which can easily be removed	**Lactic acid** which leads to muscular fatigue and pain

Lactic acid The by-product of creating energy for the muscles without oxygen which leads to pain and fatigue

Revision activity

Make a list of aerobic and anaerobic sports and activities, noting the intensity and duration of each. Identify an example of an aerobic performer and an anaerobic performer.

Figure 1.1.23 Triathletes, marathon runners and cross-country skiers all rely on high levels of aerobic fitness.

Now test yourself

1 Compare the duration of aerobic to anaerobic exercise.
2 Give two examples of anaerobic exercise.
3 Using a sporting example, describe the intensity and duration of aerobic exercise.
4 What is a disadvantage of anaerobic exercise?
5 True or false? To perform anaerobic exercise oxygen is required to create energy.
6 True or false? Aerobic activity raises heart rate and breathing rate and can be sustained for a long period of time.
7 True or false? Throwing the javelin is an anaerobic activity.

Exam practice

1 Which chamber of the heart is responsible for ejecting blood into the aorta?
   a) right atrium
   b) left atrium
   c) right ventricle
   d) left ventricle. [1]
2 What is the volume of air expired from the lungs per breath measured as?
   a) breathing frequency
   b) stroke volume
   c) tidal volume
   d) minute ventilation. [1]
3 Which of the following activities is an example of anaerobic exercise?
   a) 100 m sprint
   b) 200 m sprint
   c) discus
   d) all of the above. [1]
4 Describe the pathway of air through the body to the lungs. [4]
5 Define cardiac output and state how it can be calculated. [2]
6 Identify one role of red blood cells. [1]
7 Give one common feature of capillaries and alveoli. [1]
8 Describe the role of the diaphragm and intercostals in creating one breath in (inspiration). [2]
9 Using practical examples, compare the intensity and duration of aerobic and anaerobic exercise. [4]

Summary

- The systemic circuit transports blood to the body and back to the heart.
- The pulmonary circuit transports blood to the lungs and back to the heart.
- There are three main types of blood vessels:
  - arteries carry oxygenated blood at high pressure to the muscles and organs
  - capillaries have very thin walls to allow gaseous exchange at the muscles and organs
  - veins carry deoxygenated blood back to the heart against gravity and have pocket valves to prevent the backflow of blood.
- The heart has four chambers split into left and right side by the septum. Each side has an atrium at the top and a ventricle at the bottom divided by a valve to prevent backflow:
  - the aorta leaves the left ventricle to begin the systemic circuit, and the pulmonary artery leaves the right ventricle to start the pulmonary circuit
  - the vena cava enters the right atrium to end the systemic circuit and the pulmonary vein enters the left atrium to end the pulmonary circuit.
- Heart rate (HR) is the number of heart contractions per minute (bpm). HR is on average 72 bpm at rest.
- Stroke volume (SV) is the volume of blood ejected from the left ventricle per beat (ml).
- Cardiac output (Q) is the volume of blood ejected from the left ventricle per minute (l/min). $Q = HR \times SV$.
- Red blood cells contain haemoglobin and carry oxygen in the bloodstream.
- Air moves into the mouth and nose, down the trachea, into the bronchi and bronchioles to enter the alveoli for gaseous exchange.
- Gases move from an area of high to low concentration; oxygen into and carbon dioxide out of the bloodstream at the alveoli.
- The diaphragm and intercostals contract to increase the size of the chest cavity and decrease the lung air pressure, which causes an inspiration.
- Breathing rate (f) is the number of inspirations or expirations each minute (breaths/min). f on average is 12–15 breaths/min at rest.
- Tidal volume (TV) is the volume of air inspired or expired in one breath (ml).
- Minute ventilation (VE) is the volume of air inspired or expired each minute (l/min). $VE = f \times TV$.
- Aerobic exercise is heart-rate raising, moderate-intensity exercise over a long duration with oxygen, such as jogging.
- Anaerobic exercise is exhaustive, high-intensity exercise over a short duration without oxygen, such as sprinting. Anaerobic exercise produces lactic acid which leads to muscular fatigue and pain.

1.1e Effects of exercise on body systems

10 Short-term effects of exercise

Short-term effects of exercise

The short-term effects of exercise on the muscular, cardiovascular and respiratory systems are summarised in Table 1.1.11.

Table 1.1.11 The short-term effects of exercise

System	Short-term response	Effects	Example
Muscular	Increased muscle temperature	Increased speed of chemical reactions and energy production Increased flexibility and range of motion at a joint Decreased risk of injury	A javelin thrower would perform a warm-up to raise the muscle temperature in the shoulder. This would increase their flexibility and power when throwing the javelin
	Increased production of lactic acid	Decreased rate of chemical reactions and energy production Increased muscular fatigue and pain	A sprinter performing repeated sprints with little recovery will feel muscular fatigue and a decrease in performance over time
Cardio-vascular	Increased heart rate (HR), stroke volume (SV) and cardiac output (Q)	Increased blood flow, oxygen and nutrient delivery to the muscles Increased removal of waste HR can increase to around 200 bpm in maximal exercise SV can increase to around 200 ml	A marathon runner wearing a HR monitor would observe a resting HR around 60 bpm which would raise and level off around 140 bpm during the race
	Redistribution of blood flow to the muscles	A movement of blood flow to the muscles (80 per cent) rather than the organs (20 per cent) during exercise. This is known as the **vascular shunt**	A triathlete will require huge volumes of oxygen during exercise, supplied by the redistribution of blood flow to the working muscles
Respiratory	Increased breathing frequency (f), tidal volume (TV) and minute ventilation (VE)	Increased rate and depth of breathing to increase the volume of air for gaseous exchange	A Tour de France cyclist will demand huge volumes of oxygen for energy production, presented by the alveoli to the bloodstream
	Increased volume of oxygen to muscles	Increased oxygen availability increases energy production and waste product removal	Increased oxygen availability will mean an open water swimmer will be able to race at a higher intensity for a longer duration

> **Vascular shunt** The redistribution of blood flow. During exercise, blood flow increases to the muscles (80 per cent) due to vasodilation of the arterioles and decreases to the organs (20 per cent) due to vasoconstriction of the arterioles

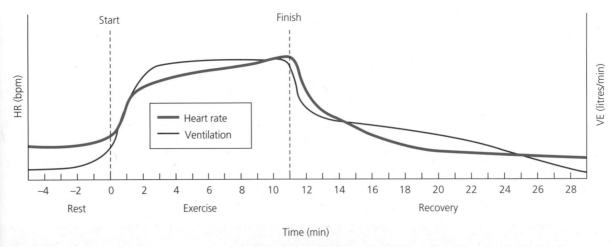

Figure 1.1.24 The short-term response of heart rate (HR) and minute ventilation (VE) to exercise.

Now test yourself

1 True or false? A short-term response of the respiratory system is increased muscle temperature.
2 True or false? Heart rate increases during exercise from a resting value on average of 72 bpm.
3 True or false? During exercise, cardiac output increases in response to an increase in heart rate and stroke volume.
4 What is the vascular shunt?
5 Describe the short-term effect of increased oxygen to the working muscles.
6 What is the consequence for an athlete of increased production of lactic acid?

Revision activity

Assess your heart rate and breathing frequency over a 60-second period while your body is at rest. In words, describe how warm or cold your muscles feel and whether you have any sensation of soreness or fatigue in your muscles. Record your results. After a warm-up, perform light aerobic exercise (for example jogging, cycling or swimming) for a period of 10 minutes. Repeat your measures and record your results again. Evaluate your short-term response to exercise and draw a graph of results. If in good health, repeat this process with anaerobic exercise and compare the results.

11 Long-term effects of exercise

Exercise can greatly affect quality of life and bring many long-term benefits. These can be considered as benefits to the skeletal and muscular, cardiovascular and respiratory systems.

Skeletal and muscular system

Table 1.1.12 The long-term effects of exercise on the skeletal and muscular system

Long-term response	Effect	Example
Increased bone density	Increased mineral density and calcium absorption to increase bone strength, decrease injury risk and protect against **osteoporosis**	The weight-bearing exercise of jogging twice a week increases bone density and strength
Hypertrophy of muscles and increased muscular strength	Increased **fast twitch muscle fibre** size leads to increased muscle strength and resistance to fatigue	Weight training three to five times a week increases muscle size as shown by Olympic weightlifters
Increased muscular endurance and resistance to fatigue	Increased **slow twitch muscle fibre** size leads to increased energy production and ability to train at a higher intensity for longer duration	A marathon runner may have slow twitch muscle fibres 22 per cent larger than average to prevent muscular fatigue

Osteoporosis A disease where the bones become brittle, fragile and easily broken

Fast twitch muscle fibre Muscle fibre which produces maximum force over a short period of time

Slow twitch muscle fibre Muscle fibre which produces a small amount of force over a long period of time

Bradycardia A resting heart rate of below 60 bpm

Capillarisation The formation and development of a network of capillaries

Cardiovascular system

Table 1.1.13 The long-term effects of exercise on the cardiovascular system

Long-term response	Effect	Examples
Hypertrophy of the heart	The heart muscle gets bigger and stronger, which increases stroke volume (SV) and allows heart rate (HR) to decrease at rest	• Endurance performers' hearts become very efficient and have **bradycardia**
Decreased resting heart rate Increased resting stroke volume	As the heart increases in size and strength, more blood can be ejected per beat and so the heart does not need to beat as often	• Triathlete Alistair Brownlee recorded a resting HR of 34 bpm • A trained Tour de France cyclist's Q may reach 20 l/min at moderate intensity compared to an untrained cyclist at 15 l/min
Increased cardiac output	During exercise increased SV leads to increased cardiac output and blood flow to the muscles to deliver oxygen and remove waste	• A well-trained 10,000 m runner will be able to train at a higher intensity for longer duration as they will resist fatigue and recover quickly
Increased speed of recovery	SV, cardiac output (Q) and blood flow are higher, therefore waste products are removed more quickly, allowing faster recovery rates	
Capillarisation	Increased number of capillaries over alveoli and muscle surfaces to increase gaseous exchange	

1.1 Applied anatomy and physiology

Respiratory system

Table 1.1.14 The long-term effects of exercise on the respiratory system

Long-term response	Effect	Examples
Increased aerobic capacity	Increased ability to breathe in, transport and use oxygen which increases the intensity and duration of performance without fatigue	• Track athlete Mo Farrah's performance is dependent on aerobic capacity and is up to 50 per cent better than an average person
Increased strength of respiratory muscles	Increased force of contraction leads to increased volume of chest cavity and lung volumes	• Endurance athletes often use deep breathing exercises to increase the strength of the diaphragm and intercostals
Increased tidal volume (TV) and minute ventilation during exercise	Increased volume of oxygen diffused into the bloodstream and removal of waste products Decreased breathing rate as TV increases	

Now test yourself

TESTED ☐

1 True or false? Bradycardia is a resting heart rate of below 60 bpm.
2 True or false? Increasing bone density has the potential to offset or delay the disease osteoporosis.
3 True or false? Aerobic capacity is decreased with long-term endurance training.
4 Describe a long-term effect of exercise on the muscles.
5 How does hypertrophy of the heart help a sports performer?
6 Name two long-term effects of exercise on the respiratory system.

Exam tip

Be prepared to identify the short-term and long-term effects of exercise but also be able to explain your answers and link them to how they help a sports performer.

Typical mistake

Read the question carefully. Make sure you identify whether the question is 'short-term' or 'long-term'. Students often give great answers but for the wrong questions.

Exam practice

1 Which of the following is a short-term effect of exercise?
   a) decreased muscle temperature
   b) decreased heart rate
   c) decreased blood flow to the organs
   d) decreased production of lactic acid. [1]
2 The delay of the disease osteoporosis is associated with which long-term effect of exercise?
   a) increased muscular endurance
   b) increased bone density
   c) capillarisation
   d) hypertrophy of the heart. [1]
3 Hypertrophy of the heart leads to which long-term effect of exercise?
   a) increased strength of the heart
   b) increased stroke volume
   c) decreased resting heart rate
   d) all of the above. [1]
4 Identify two short-term effects of exercise on the cardiovascular system. [2]
5 Describe the effect of redistributing blood flow to the muscles during exercise. [1]
6 Evaluate how the long-term effects of exercise on the respiratory system could be beneficial to a marathon runner. [3]

Summary

- The short-term effects of exercise are:
  - muscular system: increased muscle temperature and production of lactic acid
  - cardiovascular system: increased heart rate, stroke volume and cardiac output, and redistribution of blood flow to the muscles
  - respiratory system: increased breathing rate, tidal volume and minute ventilation, and increased volume of oxygen to the working muscles.
- The long-term effects of exercise are:
  - skeletal and muscular system: increased bone density, hypertrophy of muscles, increased muscular strength and increased muscular endurance
  - cardiovascular system: hypertrophy of the heart, decreased resting heart rate, increased resting stroke volume, increased cardiac output, decreased rate of recovery and capillarisation
  - respiratory system: increased aerobic capacity, increased strength of respiratory muscles, increased tidal volume and minute ventilation during exercise.

1.2 Physical training

1.2a Components of fitness

12 Components of fitness

Components of fitness

Table 1.2.1 The key components of fitness with practical examples and suitable tests

Component of fitness	Definition	Practical examples	Suitable test
Cardiovascular endurance (stamina)	The ability to continuously exercise without tiring **VO$_2$ max**: the maximum volume of oxygen taken in and used each minute	Marathon running Cross-country skiing Jogging	Cooper 12-minute run Multi-stage fitness test
Muscular endurance	The ability of a group of muscles to repeatedly contract without tiring	Rowing Cycling Swimming	Press-up test Sit-up test
Speed	The ability of the body or parts of the body to move quickly	Sprinting 50 m freestyle Cricket bowling	30 m sprint test
Strength	The ability of the muscles to exert force	Weightlifting Rugby Shot-put	Grip strength dynamometer One repetition maximum
Power	The combination of strength and speed	Triple/long/high jump Basketball Football	Standing/vertical jump test
Flexibility	The range of motion about a joint	Trampolining Dance Swimming	Sit and reach test
Agility	The ability to change direction at speed	Netball Volleyball Squash	Illinois agility test
Balance	The ability to keep a body's centre of mass over its base of support	Gymnastics Dance Martial arts	Stork stand test
Co-ordination	The ability to use different body parts together accurately and fluently	Badminton Tennis Golf	Wall throw test
Reaction time	The time taken from the stimulus to the start of a response	Sprinting Track cycling Table tennis	Reaction time ruler test

Figure 1.2.1 The multi-stage fitness test used to assess cardiovascular endurance.

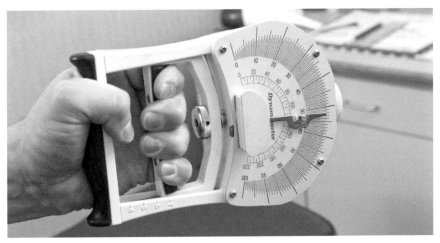

Figure 1.2.2 The handgrip dynamometer test which assesses strength.

VO$_2$ max The maximum volume of oxygen taken in and used each minute

Typical mistake

Don't get confused between cardiovascular endurance and muscular endurance. Cardiovascular endurance is a whole body measure of aerobic fitness whereas muscular endurance is specific to a group of muscles repeatedly contracting.

Exam tip

Make sure you have had a go at each of these tests so that you can describe them if required. For example, the multi-stage fitness test uses 20 m shuttle runs to a timed beep which progressively gets quicker to the point where a person can no longer keep pace. At the point of exhaustion, the level and shuttle number are recorded and VO$_2$ max is estimated from a table.

Exam tip

You may need to interpret, plot or analyse data regarding the components of fitness. Be prepared for simple calculations and know average values for each component, such as:

- cardiovascular endurance: multi-stage fitness test average VO$_2$ max 36–44 ml/kg/min (female/male 17–20 year olds)
- muscular endurance: sit-up test average 64 cumulative sit-ups
- power: vertical jump test average 40 cm
- flexibility: sit and reach test average 7–11 cm.

Now test yourself

TESTED ☐

1 True or false? Reaction time cannot be assessed.
2 True or false? Speed is assessed using the 30 m sprint test.
3 True or false? Co-ordination is assessed using the wall throw test.
4 What is an average VO$_2$ max for a 17-year-old male?
5 Give a sporting example of agility.
6 Explain why a handstand in gymnastics is an example of balance.

Exam practice

1 Which of the following is an appropriate test to assess muscular endurance?
   a) multi-stage fitness test
   b) vertical jump test
   c) Cooper 12-minute run
   d) sit-up test. [1]

2 Which of the following is the best practical example of agility?
   a) a 100 m sprinter responding to the gun and completing the race
   b) a gymnast performing a split leap on the beam
   c) a netball goal shooter performing a set piece around the goal circle to get free and receive a ball at speed
   d) a weightlifter performing a deadlift. [1]

3 Power is the combination of which two other components of fitness?
   a) speed and agility
   b) speed and strength
   c) speed and co-ordination
   d) strength and agility. [1]

4 Identify a suitable test that can be used to assess the balance of a dancer. [1]

5 Define cardiovascular endurance and explain why this component of fitness is particularly important in a sporting example of your choice. [3]

6 Evaluate the following data of a 17-year-old male and give recommendations as to which components of fitness require improvement. [5]

Test	Result
Multi-stage fitness test	30 ml/kg/min
Vertical jump test	60 cm
30 m sprint test	4.8 s
Sit and reach test	4 cm

Summary

- Cardiovascular endurance is the ability to continuously exercise without tiring, required in a marathon. It can be assessed using the multi-stage fitness test.
- Muscular endurance is the ability of a group of muscles to repeatedly contract without tiring, required in rowing. It can be assessed using the press-up test.
- Speed is the ability to move quickly, required when sprinting. It can be assessed using the 30 m sprint test.
- Strength is the ability of the muscles to exert force, required when weightlifting. It can be assessed using the one repetition maximum test.
- Power is the combination of speed and strength, required in the triple jump. It can be assessed using the vertical jump test.
- Flexibility is the range of motion about a joint, required when dancing. It can be assessed using the sit and reach test.
- Agility is the ability to change direction at speed, required when dodging in basketball. It can be assessed using the Illinois agility test.
- Balance is the ability to keep the centre of mass over the base of support, required by a gymnast on the beam. It can be assessed using the stork stand test.
- Co-ordination is the ability to use different body parts together accurately and fluently, required by a tennis player. It can be assessed using the wall throw test.
- Reaction time is the time taken from a stimulus to the start of a response, required by a track cyclist. It can be assessed using the reaction time ruler test.

1.2b Applying the principles of training

13 Principles of training

Components of fitness: SOPR

The basic building blocks of training are SOPR:

- **Specificity**: training should be relevant and appropriate for the individual, sport, muscle fibre type and movement pattern. For example, a marathon runner's training should focus on running, with slow twitch muscle fibres using continuous aerobic activity to improve cardiovascular endurance.
- **Overload**: training should push the performer beyond their comfort zone to force an adaptation. For example, a weightlifter will overload each session by increasing the weight lifted and number of repetitions and sets to increase strength.
- **Progression**: training demands should gradually increase over time to make sure that the performer improves. For example, a young gymnast should increase the intensity of training gradually to prevent injuries.
- **Reversibility**: training must be maintained to prevent a loss in performance. For example, if a cyclist becomes injured they may lose muscular endurance due to a lack of training.

> ### Revision activity
>
> Identify the main fitness component within your chosen physical activity and apply the basic principles of training to your own personal improvement.

> ### Exam tip
>
> Do not repeat the principle when describing the principles of training, for example avoid saying specificity is making training 'specific'.

Now test yourself

TESTED

1 True or false? The principle of overload ensures a performer stays within their comfort zone to prevent injury.
2 True or false? A performer should use the principles of training to ensure their training programme allows them to reach their potential.
3 True or false? Injury can cause a loss in performance if training stops.
4 Define specificity of training.
5 Give a practical example of the use of overload when designing training programmes.
6 Explain why the principle of reversibility is crucial when designing a training programme.

14 Optimising training

FITT principle

To optimise training, four components of the principle of overload can be manipulated:

- **Frequency**: how many sessions per week are performed.
- **Intensity**: how hard the sessions are.
- **Time**: how long the sessions, intervals or sets are.
- **Type**: the method of training used.

Each individual component of the **FITT principle** can be increased to maximise training, however it is common to increase only one or two at a time to prevent an athlete from burning out or risking injury. For example, for an elite 17-year-old endurance performer the general guidelines are:

- frequency: four or five days a week
- intensity: 60–80 per cent of maximum heart rate (HR_{max})
- time (distance): 3–9 miles (5–14 km) a day/15–25 miles (24–40 km) a week
- type: continuous training, circuit training and hill running.

Types of training

The correct choice of training type can maintain motivation, limit injuries and satisfy the principle of specificity:

- **Continuous training**: steady-state low–moderate-intensity exercise for a prolonged period of time. Aerobic exercise for longer than 20 minutes that is used to improve cardiovascular endurance. Typical activities involve large muscle groups: jogging, swimming, cycling and rowing.
- **Fartlek training**: continuous steady-state aerobic exercise with random higher intensity periods. Known as 'speed play', it is used to add variety to training and improve cardiovascular endurance, anaerobic fitness and recovery during lower intensity activities. Typical activities include hill running and jogging with fast sprints.
- **Interval training**: periods of exercise followed by periods of rest used by both aerobic and anaerobic performers. The intensity and duration of the exercise period and rest period can be altered for the individual. Commonly used by games players. Typical activities include jogging then walking, swimming at higher then lower intensities, and rowing then resting.

Several types of training can be classified as interval training as they use periods of work and periods of rest. These are:

- **Circuit training**: a series of exercise stations arranged in a specific order to usually alternate muscle groups. The stations can be aerobic or anaerobic, use body weight or equipment and can be performed individually or with a partner. Typical activities include star jumps, burpees, shuttle runs and dribbling exercises.
- **Weight training**: a series of exercises organised into sets of repetitions with an intensity and recovery time specific to the individual. It is used to increase strength and muscular endurance, with high weight and low repetitions used for maximum strength gains, compared to low-weight high repetitions used for muscular endurance. Typical exercises include biceps curls, triceps dips, squats, calf raises and hamstring curls.
- **Plyometrics**: a series of explosive exercises to improve the speed at which a muscle contracts. Used by performers who sprint, jump or throw to improve dynamic strength and power. Typical activities include hopping, bounding and jumping.
- **High-intensity interval training (HIIT)**: repeated periods of high-intensity exercise followed by varied recovery times. High-intensity intervals typically use 80 per cent of a person's heart rate maximum (HR_{max}) for several minutes followed by 50 per cent of HR_{max} recovery interval for a similar time. Typical activities include sprint training and hill climbing in cycling or running.

FITT principle
The component parts of the principle of training overload. Frequency, Intensity, Time and Type can all be manipulated to maximise training

Continuous training
Steady-state low–moderate intensity exercise for a prolonged period of time

Fartlek training Continuous steady-state aerobic exercise with random higher intensity periods

Interval training Periods of exercise followed by periods of rest. Includes circuit, weight, plyometric and high-intensity interval training

Revision activity

Go to your local fitness or leisure centre and participate in as many group exercise classes as possible, from weight and circuit training to HIIT. Consider the organisation of the sessions in terms of intervals of exercise and intervals of rest.

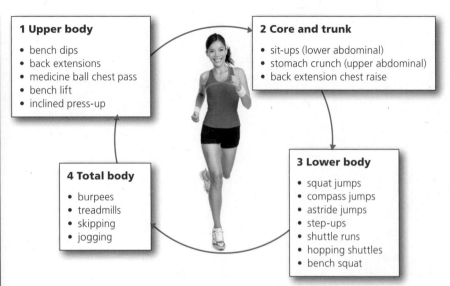

1 Upper body
- bench dips
- back extensions
- medicine ball chest pass
- bench lift
- inclined press-up

2 Core and trunk
- sit-ups (lower abdominal)
- stomach crunch (upper abdominal)
- back extension chest raise

3 Lower body
- squat jumps
- compass jumps
- astride jumps
- step-ups
- shuttle runs
- hopping shuttles
- bench squat

4 Total body
- burpees
- treadmills
- skipping
- jogging

Figure 1.2.3 An example of a circuit training session.

Warm-up

Essential at the beginning of all exercise sessions, a warm-up has five key components:

- **Pulse raising**: an activity that increases heart rate and temperature, for example jogging.
- **Mobility**: an activity that takes the joint through the full range of motion, for example arm circles.
- **Stretching**: an activity that increases the elasticity of muscles, tendons and ligaments, for example walking lunges.
- **Dynamic movements**: an activity that involves changes in speed and direction, for example shuttle runs.
- **Skill rehearsal**: an activity that mirrors game demands, for example dribbling in basketball.

The physical benefits of a warm-up include:
- Increasing the temperature of muscles which:
  - increases the speed of muscle contraction
  - increases flexibility of the muscles
  - range of motion at joints
  - pliability of tendons and ligaments
  which all help sporting technique and help to prevent injury.
- Increasing the heart rate and temperature of blood which:
  - increases gaseous exchange
  - increases blood flow
  - increases oxygen delivery
  - increases carbon dioxide removal
  which all help to maximise training intensity and duration and limit fatigue.

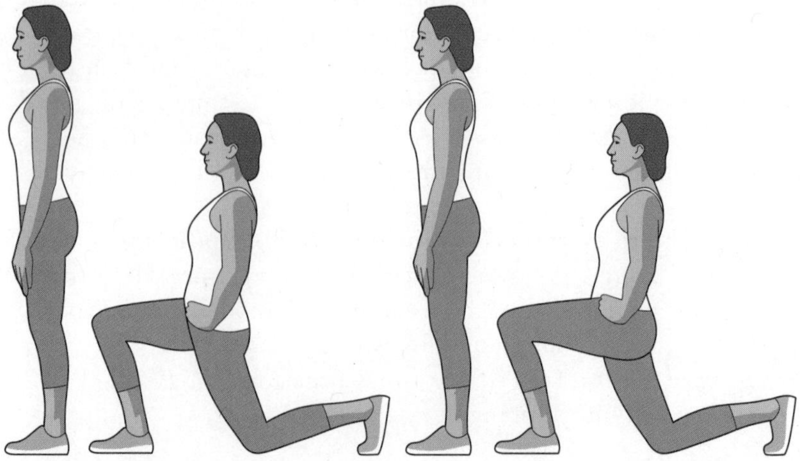

Figure 1.2.4 The warm-up and cool-down are essential elements of a fitness training session.

Cool-down

Essential at the end of all exercise sessions, a cool-down has two key components:
- **Low-intensity exercise**: an activity that gradually decreases temperature and heart and breathing rates, for example jogging.
- **Stretching**: static stretches that decrease muscle temperature, for example hamstring stretch.

The physical benefits of a cool-down include:
- The return of the body to resting state.
- The gradual lowering of heart and breathing rates which:
  - maintains blood flow
  - maintains oxygen transport
  - maintains carbon dioxide removal
  - flushes muscles with oxygenated blood to remove lactic acid
  - prevents blood pooling.
- Stretches muscles and gradually lowers muscle temperature which:
  - realigns muscle fibres
  - removes waste products
  - limits delayed onset muscle soreness.

Now test yourself

TESTED

1 True or false? The FITT principle components are frequency, intensity, type and terrain of training.
2 True or false? Plyometric training is most beneficial to endurance performers.
3 True or false? Performing a cool-down gradually lowers heart and breathing rates.
4 Give one purpose of a warm-up.
5 Give two examples of plyometric exercises.
6 Define weight training.

Exam practice

1 Which of the following is an appropriate type of training to improve cardiovascular endurance?
   a) weight training
   b) plyometrics
   c) continuous training
   d) none of the above. [1]
2 Which of the following is the best practical example of a plyometric exercise?
   a) squats
   b) shuttle runs
   c) open and close the gate
   d) jumping on and off boxes. [1]
3 Which of the following is an appropriate reason for participating in a warm-up?
   a) increase heart rate
   b) increase body temperature
   c) increase oxygen transport
   d) all of the above. [1]
4 Use your knowledge and understanding to complete the following passage. Interval training is periods of exercise followed by periods of _____. It is a common type of training used by _____ and anaerobic performers, such as games players. Circuit, _____, _____ and high intensity are all forms of interval training.
   (Word bank: continuous / aerobic / weight / plyometric / rest / fartlek.) [4]
5 Using practical examples, describe the two stages of a cool-down. [2]
6 Explain two benefits of performing a cool-down at the end of a training session. [2]

Summary

- The FIIT principle manipulates the frequency, intensity, time and type of training.
- Continuous training is steady-state low–moderate intensity exercise for a prolonged period of time.
- Fartlek training is continuous steady-state aerobic exercise with random higher intensity periods.
- Interval training is periods of exercise followed by periods of rest.
- Circuit training is a series of exercise stations arranged in a specific order to usually alternate muscle groups.
- Weight training is a series of exercises organised into sets of repetitions with an intensity and recovery time specific to the individual.
- Plyometrics is a series of explosive exercises to improve the speed at which a muscle contracts.
- High-intensity interval training (HIIT) is repeated periods of high-intensity exercise followed by varied recovery times.
- A warm-up has five components: pulse raising, mobility, stretching, dynamic movements and skill rehearsal. The benefits of a warm-up include: increasing the temperature and flexibility of the muscles, increasing the speed of muscular contraction, heart rate, blood flow and oxygen delivery.
- A cool-down has two components: low-intensity exercise and stretching. The benefits of a cool-down include: gradual decrease in heart and breathing rate, removal of lactic acid, prevention of blood pooling and limiting delayed onset muscle soreness.

1.2c Preventing injury in physical activity and training

15 Injury prevention

Minimising the risks of injury

The risk of injury in physical activity and sport can be minimised by:

- Using **personal protective equipment (PPE)**, for example gum shields to protect teeth, shin pads to protect the tibia and ankle braces to stabilise the ankle joint.
- Using the correct clothing and footwear, for example leotards in gymnastics to maximise range of motion and football boots with studs to increase grip.
- Performing in the appropriate level of competition, for example 5 km versus a full marathon for a novice versus an elite runner.
- Lifting and carrying equipment safely, for example appropriate training for setting up a trampoline or table tennis table.
- Using a warm-up and cool-down, for example a pulse raiser and dynamic stretches to prepare the body for exercise by increasing blood flow, oxygen transport and the elasticity of muscles, tendons and ligaments.

> **Personal protective equipment (PPE)**
> All equipment worn or held which protects participants from risks to their health or safety

Figure 1.2.5 The injury risk associated with roller derby is reduced by the use of personal protective equipment (PPE).

Potential hazards

A **risk assessment** can be used to identify potential **hazards** to prevent injury. Typical hazards include poor fitness, poor skill or technique, dangerous training practices or environments, weather conditions, inappropriate or damaged clothing and equipment, jewellery and the behaviour of others.

Potential hazards in specific sport settings may include:

- Sports halls: poor-quality or damaged equipment, wall surface and distance from playing area, door positions and damaged or wet floor surface.
- Fitness centres: damaged equipment, uneven or wet floor surface, lack of supervision in free weights rooms and poor fitness and technique of participants.
- Playing fields: hazards on the playing surface, damaged equipment, poor weather conditions and inappropriate footwear.
- Artificial outdoor areas: inappropriate footwear, poor weather conditions, damaged surface and poor behaviour of others.
- Swimming pools: water quality, wet surrounding surface, number of participants and poor fitness of participants.

> **Hazard** Something which has the potential to cause harm
>
> **Risk assessment** The chance of an accident occurring, anticipation of the consequences and plan of action to prevent it

Revision activity

Look around your school or college at the areas used for sports and activities. Create a table listing all the potential hazards in each area and which sports they may affect. Talk to the physical education staff about the risk assessments they have in place to prevent injuries.

Now test yourself

TESTED ☐

1 True or false? A broken leg is not a hazard found on a grass playing field.
2 True or false? A risk assessment can be used to identify potential hazards to prevent injury.
3 True or false? Personal protective equipment such as football boots with studs help to prevent injury.
4 Identify three potential hazards found in a fitness centre.
5 Identify a sporting example of requiring the need to lift or handle equipment safely.
6 What could be used to prepare the muscles for exercise before an activity begins?

Quick quizzes at **www.hoddereducation.co.uk/myrevisionnotes**

Exam practice

1 Which of the following is not an example of personal protective equipment?
   a) gum shields
   b) Lycra leotard
   c) shin pads
   d) ankle braces. [1]
2 Which of the following is the best example of a potential hazard?
   a) poor fitness
   b) poor weather conditions
   c) jewellery
   d) all of the above. [1]
3 Which of the following is a potential hazard on a playing field?
   a) lifting equipment
   b) falling over
   c) glass on the field
   d) no snacks at half time. [1]
4 Using a sporting example, describe how using the correct clothing and the appropriate footwear can reduce the risk of injury. [2]
5 Define the term hazard and give a practical example. [2]
6 Before competing at a high level, identify three key things a participant must have to prevent injury. [3]

Summary

- The risk of injury in sport can be minimised by:
  - using personal protective equipment
  - using correct clothing and footwear
  - performing at the appropriate level of competition
  - lifting and carrying safely
  - performing a warm-up and cool-down.
- A risk assessment considers the chance of an accident occurring, anticipates the consequences and creates a plan to prevent it.
- Potential hazards in physical activity and sport are:
  - poor fitness, skill, technique or training practices
  - poor environment or weather conditions
  - inappropriate or damaged clothing, equipment or jewellery
  - the behaviour of others.

2.1 Socio-cultural influences

2.1a Engagement patterns of different social groups in physical activities and sports

16 Engagement in physical activity and sport in the UK

Physical activity and sport in the UK

Current participation guidelines are:
- at least 60 minutes of moderate to vigorous physical activity each day for those aged 5–18 years
- at least 150 minutes of moderate physical activity each week for those aged 19 years and over.

Data regarding participation rates and guidelines can be found from the following organisations:
- Sport England: a national organisation working to increase participation and sporting habits for life.
- National governing bodies (NGBs): a national organisation responsible for the organisation and administration of each sport, for example the Lawn Tennis Association (LTA) and the Football Association (FA).
- Department for Culture, Media and Sport (DCMS): the government department responsible for policy related to sport.

> **Revision activity**
>
> Who is the current government minister for sport? What are their aims?

Current trends in participation in physical activity and sport

Sport participation rates are falling and obesity levels are rising. In 2016, Sport England stated that 28 per cent of people in England do less than 30 minutes of physical activity every week. Sport England's Active People Survey (2015–16) shows, by social group:
- **Age**: participation rates fall with increasing age – 56 per cent of 16–25 year olds participate in sport once a week compared to 32 per cent of over 26 year olds.
- **Gender**: men participate more than women, with around ten per cent more men than women participating in sport once a week.
- **Disability**: low but increasing participation rates, with seventeen per cent playing sport regularly.
- **Ethnicity**: participation among black and minority ethnic adults is increasing, with 37 per cent over sixteen years playing sport once a week.
- **Socio-economic status**: highest participation rates are by managerial/professional workers and lowest are by manual workers and unemployed people.

> **Exam tip**
>
> The data presented is from 2015 and 2016. Research to see if there have been changes or trends in participation rates by social group.

Figure 2.1.1 Walking football is one venture trying to maintain participation into old age.

The five most popular physical activities among adults in the UK are:
- walking
- swimming
- keep fit, yoga, aerobics or dance exercise
- cycling
- cue sports (snooker, pool and billiards).

Participation in physical activity and sport

Factors affecting participation include:
- **Age**: greatest opportunity and provision of physical activity is for school-age children. Adults see less free time, perceived lack of fitness and lack of choice. Older adults may lack confidence to participate.
- **Gender**: increased opportunity, funding and media attention for perceived male sports such as football and rugby.
- **Ethnicity, religion or culture**: worship commitments, restrictions on diet at certain times of the year and cultural beliefs may pose barriers to participation. For example, the Christian day of rest was a barrier to triple jumper Jonathan Edwards in his early career.
- **Family**: if parents are physically active it is more likely their children will be. Family support regarding money, transport and commitment may be essential for young sports performers. For example, the Cowdrey family have seen three generations represent England at cricket.
- **Education**: schools can provide a small or large number of physical activities depending on staff interest and extracurricular commitments. Equally, examination years can see a decrease in participation due to study commitments.
- **Time/work commitments**: full-time work limits time to participate, train or compete in sport.

- **Cost/disposable income**: gym memberships, facility hire, equipment cost and so on can all limit participation of certain socio-economic groups.
- **Disability**: a small number of adapted sports, lack of specialist equipment and facilities, restricted access, **discrimination** and a lack of confidence can all limit participation.
- **Opportunity/access and environment/climate**: sporting choices will depend on the opportunities on offer. Rock climbing, mountaineering, kayaking, sailing and skiing are popular sports in specific areas of the country, limiting opportunity and access to the majority.
- **Media coverage**: coverage is largely male dominated and relatively restricted to several mainstream sports such as football, rugby, tennis and athletics.
- **Role models**: the few role models promoted in minority sports can limit participation. Role models such as Beth Tweddle in gymnastics, Tom Daley in diving and Ellie Simmonds in swimming all inspire people to participate.

Strategies to improve participation include:

- **Promotion**: increase awareness of sporting opportunities, choices and role models.
- **Provision**: ensuring that the appropriate facilities, equipment and coaching are available.
- **Access**: ensuring that people can actively engage with physical activity and sport.

There are many examples of national campaigns run to increase participation in physical activity and sport. These include:

- Sport England's 'This Girl Can' is a national campaign to raise female participation and sport for all women.
- The Department of Health's 'Change4Life' included TV adverts, posters and leaflets to promote healthy eating and an active lifestyle.
- Sainsbury's 'ActiveKids' is a reward scheme for shoppers who donate sport and cooking equipment to schools to increase participation and healthy diets.

> **Discrimination** Treating a person or group of people differently – negatively or positively – due to class, gender, race, ability or sexual orientation

Figure 2.1.2 Ellie Simmonds is a fantastic role model for female participation and those with disabilities.

Figure 2.1.3 'This Girl Can' aims to raise the confidence of women to participate in physical activity and sport.

Now test yourself

1 True or false? Discrimination is the act of treating someone unfairly.
2 True or false? Sport England aims to raise participation in physical activity in sport.
3 True or false? A person's family, age and gender all affect their participation in physical activity.
4 Identify two organisations that aim to raise participation in physical activity and sport in the UK.
5 How may the environment or climate limit participation in physical activity or sport?

Exam practice

1 Which of the following matches the current physical activity guidelines in the UK for 5–18 year olds?
  a) 150 minutes of moderate physical activity per week
  b) 60 minutes of moderate to vigorous physical activity per week
  c) 60 minutes of moderate to vigorous physical activity per day
  d) 200 minutes of physical activity per week. [1]
2 Which of the following is an example of a national governing body?
  a) Youth Sports Trust
  b) Change4Life
  c) Sport England
  d) Rugby Football Union (RFU). [1]
3 Which of the following is the correct relationship between gender and participation in physical activity and sport?
  a) women participate more than men
  b) men participate more than women
  c) men and women participate equally
  d) men participate more than women but then women take over after 50 years of age. [1]
4 Identify one of the five most popular physical activities in the UK among adults. [1]
5 Identify four factors that may pose a barrier to participation in physical activity or sport. [4]
6 Describe a strategy to address gender inequality and raise the participation of women in sport. [2]

Summary

- Those aged 5–18 years old should participate in at least 60 minutes of moderate to vigorous physical activity per day.
- Those aged 19 years and over should participate in at least 150 minutes of moderate physical activity per week.
- Sport England, national governing bodies (NGBs) and the Department for Culture, Media and Sport all provide data regarding physical activity and sports participation in the UK.
- Those aged over 25 years old, women, disabled people, people from ethnic minorities and those with a low socio-economic status have lower participation in physical activity and sport than average for the UK.
- Factors affecting participation include:

  - age, gender, ethnicity, religion and culture
  - family, education and disability
  - time and work commitments, cost and disposable income
  - opportunity, access, environment and climate
  - media coverage and role models.
- Strategies to improve participation include:
  - promotion: increasing awareness of sporting opportunities, choices and role models
  - provision: ensuring the appropriate facilities, equipment and coaching are available
  - access: ensuring people can actively engage with physical activity and sport.

2.1b Commercialisation of physical activity and sport

17 Commercialisation of sport

Commercialisation and the golden triangle

Commercialisation is the process of turning something into a product to make a profit. Commercialisation of sport was the beginning of sport being run as a business.

Together, sport, media and **sponsorship** form the **golden triangle**. Sporting success brings media attention which attracts sponsorship. Media attention and sponsorship increase funding for sport. For example:

● Premier League football is a commercial success, a huge profit-making business where leagues and matches are shown through all media outlets from magazine subscriptions to live matches. Individual players, clubs and stadiums are sponsored for the financial gain it brings to the company.
● The money invested through sponsorship and the media enables the standard of players, facilities, coaching and management to be the best possible. This creates success and entertainment which keeps the media and sponsors happy.

> **Commercialisation**
> The process of running sport as a business to make a profit
>
> **Sponsorship** The funding of individuals, teams or kits to make a profit
>
> **Golden triangle**
> The relationship between and interdependence of the media, sport and sponsorship

Figure 2.1.4 The golden triangle sees Premiership football clubs being run as profit-making businesses.

Media and commercialisation

The media has a huge influence on the commercialisation of sport. There are four main types of media:

● **Television or visual**: live coverage, documentaries, news, quiz shows and advertising, for example BBC, ITV, Sky and BT Sport.
● **Social**: websites and applications that help people to create, share and discuss content, for example Facebook, Twitter, WhatsApp and forums.

- **Internet**: a place for publishing governing body rules, facts, player details, club results and so on, for example England Netball (www.englandnetball.co.uk).
- **Newspapers and magazines**: scores, factual updates, analysis and discussion, for example *The Guardian* or football's *FourFourTwo* magazine.

Table 2.1.1 The positive and negative effects of the media on the commercialisation of sport

	Positive effects	Negative effects
Influence of media on the commercialisation of sport	Increases participation Generates funding Makes sport more entertaining Makes games fairer 24-hour worldwide coverage Increases national pride Promotes minority sports Promotes good role models and breaks stereotypes Creates sports stars on and off field	Too much focus on sport: people would rather watch than participate Pay per view limits access Poor role models highlighted Damaging press coverage: intrusion into players' personal lives, pre-match hype and negativity towards opponents Minority sports have limited coverage Controls or changes sport
Practical examples	London 2012 Olympics widely covered in the media and generated huge public support inspiring people to participate	Focus on football in the UK highlighting violence and hype about rival teams, for example England versus Germany

Sponsorship and commercialisation

Sponsorship is the funding of individuals, teams or kits to make a profit.

Table 2.1.2 The positive and negative effects of sponsorship on the commercialisation of sport

	Positive effects	Negative effects
Influence of sponsorship on the commercialisation of sport	Increased funding Allows full-time training Gives financial security Pays for competitions or facilities	Bad image for sport if linked to fast food or alcohol Pressure of sponsor demands Only a few or top sports/top teams receive sponsorship Sponsorship easily lost
Practical examples	The airline Emirates has a sponsorship deal with Arsenal Football Club and has the naming rights to the Emirates Stadium: this provides the club with additional income	One of the top Olympic sponsors was fast-food chain McDonald's which some claim creates a negative image for sport

Exam tip

Make sure you understand the difference between media and sponsorship and look carefully for the indicator in the question.

Revision activity

Can you identify several examples of sponsors in sport: an individual athlete sponsor, a team sponsor, a kit sponsor or a stadium sponsor?

Now test yourself

1 True or false? Sponsorship is the funding of individuals, teams or kits to make a profit.
2 True or false? The golden triangle refers to the relationship between and interdependence of funding, ethics and commercialisation.
3 True or false? The Emirates Stadium is a good example of the media in sport.
4 Give an example of the use of social media in sport.
5 Give two positive effects of the media on the commercialisation of sport.
6 Identify two negative effects of sponsorship on the commercialisation of sport.

Exam practice

1 Which of the following is an example of sponsorship in sport?
   a) *FourFourTwo* magazine subscription
   b) the words 'Standard Chartered' on Liverpool's football kit
   c) BBC coverage of the Olympic games
   d) discussion of tactics used post-match. [1]
2 Which of the following is the correct definition of sponsorship in sport?
   a) the process of running sport as a business
   b) the promotion of sport through advertising
   c) the receiving of money to promote sport
   d) the funding of sport: individuals, teams or kits to make a profit. [1]
3 Which of the following is a positive effect of the media on the commercialisation of sport?
   a) increased participation
   b) increased funding
   c) increased entertainment
   d) all of the above. [1]
4 Define the golden triangle. [1]
5 Using a sporting example, describe a positive effect of sponsorship on the commercialisation of sport. [2]
6 Using a sporting example, explain how the media can have a negative effect on the commercialisation of sport. [3]

Summary

- Commercialisation of sport is the process of running sport as a business to make a profit.
- The golden triangle is the relationship between and interdependence of the media, sport and sponsorship.
- The media has four main types; television, social, internet and newspapers/magazines.
- The positive effects of the media on the commercialisation of sport include:
  – increased participation, funding, entertainment, fairness, coverage and national pride
  – promotion of minority sports, good role models and breaking of stereotypes.
- The negative effects of the media on the commercialisation of sport include:
  – too much focus on sport, pay-per-view access only, highlight of poor role models and damaging press coverage.

- Sponsorship is the funding of individuals, teams or kits to make a profit.
- The positive effects of sponsorship on the commercialisation of sport include:
  – increased funding, allows full-time training, financial security and competition or facility funding.
- The negative effects of sponsorship on the commercialisation of sport include:
  – negative image for sport if linked to fast food or alcohol, pressure of sponsor demands, easy withdrawal of sponsorship and limited sponsorship to the best only.

2.1c Ethical and socio-cultural issues in physical activity and sport

18 Ethical and socio-cultural issues in physical activity and sport

Ethics in sport

Sportsmanship is fair play, a behaviour that follows the written and unwritten rules of a sport. Examples of sportsmanship would be shaking hands with your opponent and then the umpire in tennis, swapping shirts at the end of a football match, and accepting an umpire's decision and continuing to play quickly in hockey.

Sportsmanship helps to:
- make an activity enjoyable
- encourage a good atmosphere and friendliness
- support the officials and umpires and helps the game to flow
- raise the status of the sport and provide good role models.

> **Sportsmanship** Behaviour that shows fair play, respect for opponents, umpires and spectators, and gracious behaviour in victory or loss
>
> **Gamesmanship** Bending of the rules to gain an unfair advantage
>
> **Deviance** Cheating. Behaviour against the written and unwritten rules of the sport, often illegal in nature

Figure 2.1.5 Sportsmanship raises the status of sport.

Gamesmanship is the bending of the rules to gain an unfair advantage in sport. Examples include whispering in a player's ear to distract them from scoring from a corner in football or pausing the server in tennis to untie and re-tie your shoelaces when your shoes were not really loose.

Deviance in sport is cheating – breaking the rules, often with illegal behaviour. Examples include taking anabolic steroids to throw further in athletics or using a two-footed tackle to deliberately foul and endanger an opponent in football.

Players can resort to gamesmanship or deviance in sport because of:
- wanting an unfair advantage over the competition
- the importance of winning a high-status competition (for example a cup final)
- pressure from fans, team-mates or sponsors.

> **Typical mistake**
>
> Do not fall into the mistake of describing gamesmanship as cheating. It is bending the rules to gain an unfair advantage.

Figure 2.1.6 Cyclist Lance Armstrong is one of the world's most famous drug cheats in sporting history.

Drugs in sport

Sports performers may use drugs for many reasons, including:

- to improve physical function, such as: build muscle, train harder, lose weight or reduce pain
- to improve psychological function, such as: steady nerves, increase motivation, alertness or aggression
- to win at all costs as a result of the fear of losing, money, glory or fame
- the belief that other performers are doing the same or the belief that they can get away with it.

Table 2.1.3 Three typical drugs used in sport with the effects on performance and side effects

Type of drug	Example	Effects on performance	Negative side effects
Anabolic steroids	Weightlifters, throwers, sprinters and 50 m swimmers	Increased muscle mass and strength Increased speed of recovery Increased intensity and duration of training	Aggression and mood swings Acne and hormonal problems Liver damage and heart failure
Beta-blockers	Snooker, archery and shooting	Decrease blood pressure, heart rate, muscle tremors and anxiety	Dry mouth, dizzy spells, tiredness and stomach problems
Stimulants	Motor sport drivers, sprinters and long-distance cyclists	Increased alertness, focus and concentration Increased use of fats and endurance of performance	Sleep problems and anxiety Stomach problems

The impact of drug use in sport can affect both the athlete and the sport itself. In addition to the side effects listed in Table 2.1.3 there are impacts on performers and sport in general.

Impact on performers

- Receive bans and fines, and be stripped of medals and titles.
- Lose sponsorship deals, respect and careers.
- Become bad role models and a national disgrace (for example Lance Armstrong).
- Break the laws of sport and laws of the land, as using drugs in sport is deviant behaviour.

Impact on sport

- Non-drug-using 'clean' athletes and new records can be questioned.
- Creates bad publicity and a bad name for the sport (for example Tour de France cycling).
- Creates a bad name for a specific country (for example China's swimming team of the 1990s).
- Drug testing, accusations and convictions are an expensive and lengthy process.

Violence in sport

Violence in sport is a common occurrence. There have been many examples:
- Ben Flower's punch of Lance Hohaia in the 2014 Rugby Super League Grand Final between local rivals.
- Zinedine Zidane's head-butting of Marco Materazzi in football's 2006 FIFA World Cup Final.
- Body checking in ice hockey.

The reasons for player violence in sport include:
- Anger or frustration at poor officiating, bad refereeing decisions, lack of time, poor score or poor performance.
- Emotional intensity of an important game, a local derby or rival, pre-match hype or rowdy spectators causing tension in the stadium.
- Abuse or provocation can cause retaliation from gamesmanship behaviour, another player's deviance, a hostile crowd or a bad tackle.
- Lack of discipline in sport, lack of punishments, players can get away with it or copying behaviour of role models.
- Nature of the game as a result of body contact, checking and rules of the game (for example ice hockey), equipment which can be used as weapons (for example sticks in hockey) and kit that de-humanises players (for example American football).

> **Revision activity**
>
> Research player violence in your sport. Are there sports which regularly see player violence and sports which have never seen participant violence? What could be the reasons for this?

Figure 2.1.7 Violence is a common occurrence with ice hockey players.

Now test yourself

1 True or false? Gamesmanship is fair play in sport.
2 True or false? The nature and rules of a sport can lead to player violence.
3 True or false? Beta-blockers are taken by an athlete to build muscle.
4 Give a sporting example of deviant behaviour.
5 Using sporting examples, identify two reasons for player violence in sport.
6 Identify two reasons why a performer may use drugs in sport.

Exam practice

1 Which of the following is an example of gamesmanship?
   a) swapping shirts at the end of a rugby match
   b) using anabolic steroids to enhance performance in athletics
   c) delaying play by changing rackets unnecessarily in tennis
   d) thanking the referee at the end of a football match.   [1]
2 Which of the following performers is most likely to abuse anabolic steroids?
   a) weightlifters
   b) cross-country skiers
   c) archers
   d) 800 m runners.   [1]
3 Which of the following could lead to a performer becoming frustrated and violent?
   a) poor referring decision
   b) match time running out
   c) losing by two goals
   d) all of the above.   [1]
4 Using a sporting example, describe a situation where a player may retaliate with violence in sport. [1]
5 What are the consequences of drug use in sport on the sport itself?   [2]
6 Using sporting examples, explain the difference between gamesmanship and deviance in sport. [3]

Summary

- Sportsmanship is fair play and makes an activity enjoyable, supports officials, raises the status of sport and provides good role models.
- Gamesmanship is bending the rules to gain an unfair advantage, whereas deviance is cheating, behaviour against the rules of the sport and often illegal.
- Drugs in sport may be used to:
  - improve physical function (for example to build muscle)
  - improve psychological function (for example to steady nerves)
  - win at all costs or because everyone else is believed to be using drugs.
- Anabolic steroids increase muscle mass, strength and power.

- Beta-blockers decrease heart rate, muscle tremors and anxiety.
- Stimulants increase alertness, focus and concentration.
- Consequences of drug use by performers: increased aggression, tiredness and anxiety, stomach problems, liver damage and heart failure. They may receive bans and fines, lose sponsorship and become a bad role model.
- Consequences of drug use for the sport: bad publicity, less respect, national disgrace and a waste of time and money.
- Violence in sport may occur due to anger or frustration, emotional intensity, abuse or provocation, lack of discipline and the nature of the game and equipment used.

2.2 Sports psychology

19 Characteristics of skilful movement and skill classification

Skilful movement

A **motor skill** is an action or a task that has a target or goal and requires voluntary limb or body movement to achieve it.

Skilful movement can be seen when a predetermined goal or target is accomplished with maximum efficiency and with the minimum output of energy. The characteristics of skilful movement include:

- **Fluent**: the skill is performed in one flowing movement. For example, a gymnast performs a cartwheel and backward walkover without stopping.
- **Efficient**: a skill is performed without wasting time or energy. For example, a swimmer uses a perfect technique in the freestyle to move through the water without energy in the fastest time possible.
- **Predetermined**: a skill has a clear objective or goal. For example, a dancer knows the routine well before starting.
- **Aesthetic**: the skill looks pleasing to the eye. For example, a dancer performs a split leap with technique that looks good.
- **Co-ordinated**: the skill is performed with control, using limbs, senses and movements at the same time. For example, a tennis player can successfully throw, hit and jump when serving.

Skill classification

Skills are classified on continua (scales) of difficulty and environmental conditions.

The **difficulty continuum** ranges from simple to complex skills. The more judgements and decisions a performer has to make to perform the skill, the more complex it becomes. It will be closer to the complex end of the difficulty continuum. For example, a netball interception is a complex skill (many decisions) compared to a sprint start in athletics which is a simple skill (few decisions).

The **environmental continuum** ranges from closed to open skills. The more affected by the environment a skill is, the more open the skill becomes. It will be closer to the open end of the environmental continuum. For example, a pass in football is an open skill as the environment is constantly changing and so movements have to be adapted, compared to a serve in tennis which is a closed skill.

Motor skill An action or task with a target requiring voluntary limb and/or body movement to achieve it

Difficulty continuum A classification scale to rate how simple or complex a skill is

Environmental continuum A classification scale to rate how open/closed or affected by the environment a skill is

---

Exam tip

Try to create a way to remember the five characteristics of skilful movement, for example the acronym FEPAC (Fluent, Efficient, Predetermined, Aesthetic and Co-ordinated).

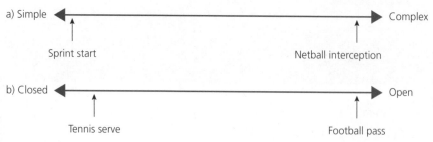

Figure 2.2.1 Sporting examples on a) the difficulty continuum and b) the environmental continuum.

Now test yourself

1 True or false? Jerkiness is a characteristic of skilful movement.
2 True or false? A motor skill is an action or task with a target requiring voluntary limb and/or body movement to achieve it.
3 True or false? Open to closed skills are classified using the difficulty continuum.
4 How would you classify a pass in rugby on both the difficulty and environmental continua?
5 Give a practical example of the characteristic of 'aesthetic' when describing skilful movement.

20 Goal setting

REVISED

Goal setting

Goal setting can be used to:

- **Adhere to exercise**. A goal can push people to stick with an exercise programme. For example, attend all three training sessions this week and you should hit your target of 1 kg weight loss.
- **Motivate performers**. A goal can inspire and drive performers to achieve their potential. For example, a weightlifter's goal of completing one additional repetition per set drives them to go further.
- **Improve or optimise performance**. A goal can lead to a higher level of performance over time. For example, a coach gives an athlete a goal to knock off 0.5 seconds from their 400 m lap time.

Goals can be related to the performance or outcome:

- Performance goals are directed to the performance or technique of the activity. For example, to toss the ball higher to give more time to accurately serve in tennis.
- Outcome goals are directed to the end result. For example, the tennis serve lands in or out.

The **SMART principle** is a useful tool to ensure the goals are appropriate and effective. There are five principles to follow when giving an athlete or a performer a goal:

- **Specific**. Goals should be clear and focused. For example, a performer on a weight loss exercise programme has a goal of losing 2 cm from their waist circumference after six weeks of aerobic exercise.
- **Measurable**. Goals should be assessed to know how well a performer has done. For example, a coach should be able to measure how many times a gymnast completes a cartwheel with perfect technique.

> **Revision activity**
>
> Draw a horizontal line. Label as the difficulty continuum with simple skills at one end and complex skills at the other. Position as many sporting examples as you can along this continuum and justify their placement. Repeat for the environmental continuum.

> **SMART principle** A useful tool to ensure goals are Specific, Measurable, Achievable, Recorded and Timed

- **Achievable**. Goals should be realistic and within the performer's capability. For example, if a netball team scored 12 goals in the first quarter a goal of 13 in the second quarter is achievable, whereas a goal of 22 goals may not be.
- **Recorded**. Measurements should be logged to track progress and adapt training programmes and future goals to suit progress. For example, a weightlifter records the number of sets, reps and weight lifted each session to ensure there is progress.
- **Timed**. Short-term goals are more achievable and lead up to long-term goals. For example, a one-week goal for training to improve the sprint-start technique.

Now test yourself

TESTED

1 True or false? 'Accurate' is part of the SMART principle of goal setting.
2 True or false? Outcome goals are focused towards the performance or technique of the activity.
3 True or false? Effective goal setting can motivate performers.
4 Identify three of the five elements of the SMART principle of goal setting.
5 Using a sporting example, describe how goal setting can help a performer to adhere to training.

21 Mental preparation

REVISED

Mental preparation is used by those who participate in a physical activity and sport to cope with high levels of stress and **anxiety**.

Mental preparation techniques

The key mental preparation techniques are as follows:
- **Imagery**: the creation of pictures in a performer's mind to get a feeling of the movement, relax or get a feeling of pleasure. For example, a footballer before a cup final may think of a calm, relaxing place to quell their nerves.
- **Mental rehearsal**: going through the activity in your mind to form a mental image of the skill about to be performed. This can help to learn a new skill, improve existing skills and control anxiety. This can be:
  - **Internal imagery**: imagining yourself doing the activity. For example, a gymnast imagining themselves performing the routine and feeling when to go into and out of specific movements.
  - **External imagery**: picturing yourself doing the activity from outside your body. For example, a racing driver imagining driving the course from outside the car.
- **Selective attention**: when a performer concentrates on relevant information and ignores distractions. For example, a golfer tries to filter out the noise of the crowd and movement of objects around them to focus on the ball and shot they are about to play.
- **Positive thinking**: positive thinking or self-talk is when performers talk to themselves or think positively about past performances to increase self-confidence about future efforts. For example, a footballer preparing to take a penalty says to herself, 'you can do it, you've done it so many times before, remember that time you put it in the top right-hand corner to win the match?'

Anxiety A feeling of fear that we experience that something might go wrong either in the present or in the future

Revision activity

Next time you are preparing to compete or participate in sport or a physical activity, try using each of the key mental preparation techniques before you start, during stoppages, at half time or in a break in play. Consider how it makes you feel and if you have a preference for one type of mental preparation.

Figure 2.2.2 A golfer using mental rehearsal to go through his shot to control anxiety.

Now test yourself

TESTED

1 True or false? Selective attention is the ability to ignore distractions and focus on relevant information.
2 True or false? Thinking positively can increase self-confidence.
3 True or false? Internal imagery is picturing yourself performing an activity from outside your body.
4 State four mental preparation techniques.
5 Using a sporting example, describe mental rehearsal.

22 Types of guidance and feedback

REVISED

Guidance

Guidance is essential when a coach or instructor teaches a new skill to a novice or develops the skills of an experienced performer. There are several types of guidance:

- **Visual**: uses a demonstration, video, chart or illustration to build an 'ideal' picture of what is required to correctly perform a skill.
- **Verbal**: describes or explains how to perform a skill. Mostly used in conjunction with visual guidance to reinforce a mental picture.
- **Manual**: gives physical support from a coach or an instructor to guide the performer.
- **Mechanical**: uses equipment to guide and support a performer.

> **Revision activity**
>
> Write down an example in your sport where your coach has used each type of guidance.

Table 2.2.1 The advantages and disadvantages of different types of guidance method

Type of guidance	Practical example	Advantages	Disadvantages
Visual	Demonstration of a penalty flick in hockey	Good for beginners Easy to remember Technical model to copy Quick and effective	Hard to get a feel for the skill if the demonstration is incorrect, too complicated or overloads information
Verbal	Coach telling a goal attack in netball to move up court to receive a ball	Immediate and quick Fine tuning or developing skilled movements Can be used alongside visual guidance	Hard to create a mental picture if the information is incorrect, confusing or overloads information
Manual	A coach supporting the leg as a dancer performs an arabesque	Reduces fear in dangerous situations Increases safety Raises confidence Gives a kinaesthetic feel to the performer	Unrealistic feeling of the skill or **kinaesthesis** Overreliance on the support Dangerous if incorrect
Mechanical	A novice swimmer using a float		

Figure 2.2.3 Manual guidance effectively supporting the gymnast in the early stages of learning a handstand.

Kinaesthesis
The awareness or feeling a performer gets through movement as proprioceptors in the muscles, ligaments and joints send information to the brain

Exam tip

The advantages and disadvantages for manual guidance are the same as those for mechanical guidance.

Feedback

Feedback can motivate, change performance and reinforce learning. For feedback to be effective, it needs to be accurate, understandable and given in a timely manner. There are six main types of feedback:

- **Intrinsic feedback**: continuous from within the performer. For example, a gymnast performing a handstand feels that their legs are straight.
- **Extrinsic feedback**: comes from external sources such as sound or vision. For example, a netball goalkeeper sees the ball go into the net.
- **Knowledge of performance**: feedback about how well a movement is executed. For example, a ski coach tells the skier their weight is in the correct place as they move around the slalom pole.

- **Knowledge of results**: feedback about the end result of a response. For example, a gymnast lands the dismount from the vault well.
- **Positive feedback**: reinforces skill learning and gives information about successful outcomes. For example, a coach praises a footballer for a correct pass.
- **Negative feedback**: gives information about unsuccessful outcomes and can be used to build strategies. For example, a tennis coach telling a player their grip is incorrect.

Now test yourself

TESTED

1 True or false? Visual guidance uses demonstrations, videos or charts to build a mental picture of a correctly performed skill.
2 True or false? The advantages and disadvantages for manual guidance are the same as those for mechanical guidance.
3 True or false? Knowledge of results gives information about how well a movement is executed.
4 What is the difference between positive and negative feedback?
5 Describe a practical example where mechanical guidance is important.

Exam practice

1 Which of the following is the best example of a skilled performer showing a fluent characteristic?
   a) a tennis player performing a serve and immediately continuing to volley at the net
   b) a footballer taking a penalty
   c) a javelin thrower assessing their performance
   d) a gymnast receiving feedback from their coach. [1]
2 Which of the following is an example of an open skill?
   a) a tennis serve
   b) a darts throw
   c) a hockey pass
   d) a gymnastic jump on the beam. [1]
3 'An action or task with a target requiring voluntary limb and/or body movement to achieve it' is a definition of what?
   a) skill classification
   b) skill continua
   c) skilful movement
   d) motor skill. [1]
4 Which type of guidance is the coach using when they give physical support?
   a) mechanical guidance
   b) visual guidance
   c) manual guidance
   d) mechanical and manual guidance. [1]

5 Which type of feedback is a coach giving if they say: 'you hit the backboard too high so the ball missed the basket'?
   a) positive
   b) extrinsic
   c) negative
   d) intrinsic. [1]
6 Giving sporting examples of motor skills, describe a closed skill and a complex skill. [2]
7 Using sporting examples, describe and explain the difficulty continuum of skill classification. [2]
8 Identify one use of goal setting for a sports performer. Using a sorting example, describe how three aspects of the SMART principle may help to ensure the goals are appropriate and effective. [4]
9 Using a sporting example, describe the use of selective attention as a mental preparation technique. [1]
10 Give an example of visual guidance and identify one advantage and one disadvantage of its use. [3]
11 Compare knowledge of performance to knowledge of results. [2]
12 Outline the difference between manual and mechanical guidance. Using sporting examples, give two reasons why manual and mechanical guidance can be important to learning skills. [2]

Summary

- A motor skill is an action or task with a target requiring voluntary limb and/or body movement to achieve it.
- The main characteristics of skilful movement are Fluent, Efficient, Predetermined, Aesthetic and Co-ordinated (FEPAC).
- The difficulty continuum classifies simple to complex skills. The more judgements and decisions a performer has to make the more complex the skill becomes.
- The environmental continuum classifies closed to open skills. The more affected by the environment a skill is the more open the skill becomes.
- Goal setting can increase exercise adherence and motivation, and optimise performance.
- The SMART principle ensures that goals are Specific, Measurable, Achievable, Recorded and Timed.
- The key mental preparation techniques are:
  - imagery: the creation of pictures in a performer's mind
  - mental rehearsal: going through the activity in your mind to form a mental image of the skill
  - selective attention: concentrating on relevant information and ignoring distractions
  - positive thinking: self-talk or focusing on successful past performances.

- Visual guidance uses a demonstration to create a mental picture of how to perform a skill. This is good for beginners and easy to remember, however, it is hard to get a feel for the skill and the demonstration must be correct.
- Verbal guidance describes or explains how to perform a skill. This is immediate and can fine-tune a skill, however, it is hard to create a mental picture and the information must be correct.
- Manual guidance gives physical support to the performer.
- Mechanical guidance uses equipment to support the performer. Manual and mechanical guidance increase safety and confidence, however, the feeling can be unrealistic and the performer can begin to rely on the support.
- Intrinsic feedback comes from within the performer.
- Extrinsic feedback comes from external sources.
- Knowledge of performance gives feedback about how well a movement was executed.
- Knowledge of results gives feedback about the end result of a response.
- Positive feedback gives information about successful outcomes.
- Negative feedback gives information about unsuccessful outcomes.

2.3 Health, fitness and well-being

23 Health, fitness and well-being

REVISED

Leading a healthy, balanced lifestyle can help you to feel better and live longer. There are three key aspects:

- **Health**: a state of complete physical, mental and social well-being. Not just the absence of disease or infirmity.
- **Fitness**: a person's capacity to carry out life's activities without getting too tired. The body's ability to function efficiently and effectively.
- **Well-being**: the feeling or mental state of being contented, happy, prosperous and healthy.

Healthy, balanced lifestyle

A healthy, balanced lifestyle as defined in the UK includes:

- a healthy and balanced diet
- regular exercise
- maintaining a healthy body weight
- not smoking and not drinking alcohol excessively
- minimising stress
- maintaining positive relationships.

Physical activity and sport can have many health benefits in terms of a person's physical, emotional and social well-being, whereas leading a **sedentary** lifestyle can lead to severe consequences.

> **Health** A state of complete physical, emotional and social well-being
>
> **Fitness** The body's ability to function efficiently and effectively
>
> **Well-being** Positive mental state of being happy and healthy
>
> **Sedentary** Inactive and spending a large proportion of the day sitting down

Physical issues

Table 2.3.1 **The health benefits of physical activity and sedentary consequences on physical function**

Benefits of physical activity and sport	Consequences of a sedentary lifestyle
Prevents injury, for example by increasing the flexibility and stability of joints	Increases risk of injury, for example poor joint flexibility and stability
Decreases the risk of coronary heart disease (CHD) and high blood pressure, for example by decreasing blood fats, increasing blood flow and circulation	Increases risk of CHD and high blood pressure, for example by reduced blood flow, poor circulation and poor removal of fats in the bloodstream
Increases and maintains bone density, for example stimulates new bone growth to withstand stress	Low bone density, for example lack of bone growth or renewal which increases the chance of fractures
Prevents obesity and limits type 2 diabetes, for example body fat and blood sugars are used when exercising	Leads to obesity and type 2 diabetes, for example low energy levels, stored body fat and high circulating levels of blood sugar
Increases fitness and maintains a good posture, for example increases energy levels and strengthens core muscles to prevent lower back pain	Poor fitness and posture, for example low energy levels, weakness, easily out of breath and a weak core which can lead to lower back pain

Emotional issues

Table 2.3.2 The health benefits of physical activity and sedentary consequences on emotional well-being

Benefits of physical activity and sport	Consequences of a sedentary lifestyle
Increases self-esteem and confidence, for example exercise releases endorphins (types of hormones) that elevates mood, increases life skills to experience success and achieve goals	Decreases self-esteem and confidence, for example poor body image
Good management of stress, for example stress can be relieved through exercise and endorphins are released	Poor management of stress, for example lack of ways to release stress
A positive body image, for example by being happy with physique which raises self-esteem and confidence	Negative body image, for example negative feelings about body shape or size can decrease self-esteem and confidence

Social issues

Table 2.3.3 The health benefits of physical activity and sedentary consequences on social well-being

Benefits of physical activity and sport	Consequences of a sedentary lifestyle
Increases friendship group, for example opportunity to meet new people, share experiences and work cooperatively	Small friendship group, for example potential lack of social interaction or opportunities to develop friendships
Increases sense of belonging, for example opportunity to feel part of a team in a running club, football team or exercise class	Feeling isolated, for example potential to feel isolated and not part of a community
Socially active, for example increased opportunities for social gatherings, occasions and interactions, for example matches, training sessions and awards evenings	Loneliness, for example potential isolation, lack of people to talk to and interact with

Figure 2.3.1 Participation in group activity or team sports can increase a person's friendship group and sense of belonging and keep them socially active into later life.

Ageing

The impacts of age include the following:

- The effects of a sedentary lifestyle on physical function accumulate with age, with people beginning to see a negative impact after their 30s.
- The emotional and social consequences of inactivity can occur during a working life when people have little time to participate. This also occurs during the elderly years when there are potentially fewer opportunities to participate.
- The easiest time for social benefits from physical activity and sport is during education when people's free time and access to opportunities are highest.

Now test yourself

TESTED

1 True or false? To be healthy is to be in a complete state of physical, emotional and social well-being.
2 True or false? A sedentary lifestyle is one where an individual gains benefits in physical, emotional and social well-being from participating in physical activity and sport.
3 True or false? When you are physically active your body releases hormones which raise your mood.
4 Identify three potential health benefits of participating in physical activity and sports on physical function.
5 Identify two sedentary consequences of not participating in physical activity or sport on emotional well-being.
6 Why might a sedentary lifestyle lead to decreased self-esteem or confidence?

24 Diet and nutrition

REVISED

A balanced diet involves eating a wide variety of food including five portions of fruit and vegetables a day to allow the body to function efficiently and effectively. This diet should contain approximately 55 per cent carbohydrates, 15 per cent proteins and no more than 30 per cent fats.

Components of a balanced diet

The components of a balanced diet are:

- **Carbohydrates**: simple sugars (fruit juice and honey) and complex starches (pasta and potatoes) are essential for energy production. They circulate in the blood as glucose and are stored in the muscles and liver as glycogen. Carbohydrates account for up to 75 per cent of energy requirements in physical activity and sport.
- **Proteins**: found in meat and fish are essential for growth and repair and the production of haemoglobin. Proteins aid the recovery and repair after a heavy weight training session.
- **Fats**: insulate, cushion organs and provide an energy store. Fats are a source of energy for endurance performers, for example triathletes.
- **Vitamins and minerals**: essential nutrients. Vitamins are required for blood clotting and eye, skin, connective tissue and bone health. Minerals are required to make haemoglobin, and for bone health and energy production. Vitamin C is important for blood vessels, tendons, ligaments and bone health.

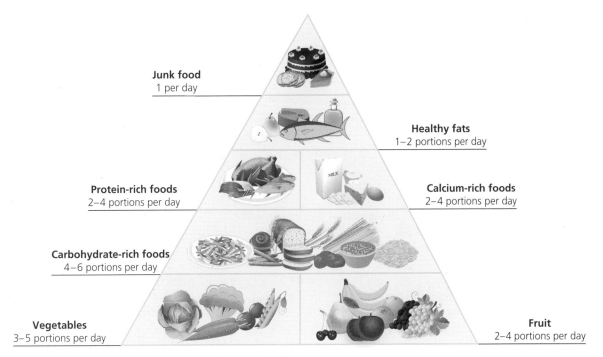

Figure 2.3.2 Daily composition of a balanced diet.

- **Fibre**: found in cereals and beans helps the large intestine to function normally. Coupled with exercise, good dietary fibre helps to reduce the risk of diabetes and obesity.
- **Water and hydration**: essential to allow chemical reactions and to dissolve and move substances around the body. Adequate hydration is essential before, during and after training, especially in hot conditions and endurance activities, for example marathon running.

The effect of diet and hydration on energy use in physical activity:

- An athlete's diet should be in energy balance. Their intake of energy through food and drinks should match the energy they use to train, perform and live their daily lives. If the energy balance is incorrect, the athlete will either start to lose weight (possibly muscle) or gain weight (possibly fat).
- Carbohydrate loading in the lead-up to an event maximises carbohydrate (glycogen) stores to increase energy production and delay fatigue.
- Sports drinks contain sugar (glucose) and salts (electrolytes) which can be used to top up energy stores during training and prevent dehydration.
- Dehydration leads to decreased stroke volume, raised heart rate and thicker blood. This puts a greater strain on the heart and uses energy more quickly, leading to early fatigue.

Now test yourself

TESTED ☐

1 True or false? Carbohydrates are essential for growth and repair and the production of haemoglobin.
2 True or false? Dietary fibre and exercise can reduce the risk of diabetes and obesity.
3 True or false? An energy balance is achieved when energy intake equals energy output.
4 Define a balanced diet.
5 Why is water an important part of the diet?
6 Why would an athlete maximise carbohydrate stores before a competition?

Exam practice

1 Which of the following is not a part of a healthy, balanced lifestyle?
   a) regular exercise
   b) limiting alcohol intake
   c) five portions of fruit and vegetables a day
   d) absorbing stress. [1]
2 Which of the following is an example of a health benefit of physical activity on emotional well-being?
   a) increased fitness
   b) improve and maintain good posture
   c) positive body image
   d) increased friendship group. [1]
3 Which of the following is the correct composition of a healthy diet?
   a) 40 per cent carbohydrates, 35 per cent protein and no more than 25 per cent fats
   b) 55 per cent carbohydrates, 15 per cent protein and no more than 30 per cent fats
   c) 70 per cent carbohydrates, 20 per cent protein and no more than 10 per cent fats
   d) 55 per cent carbohydrates, 25 per cent protein and no more than 20 per cent fats. [1]
4 Using a sporting example, describe a health benefit of physical activity on social well-being. [1]
5 Using sporting examples, why are carbohydrates and proteins an essential part of the athlete's diet? [2]
6 Describe and explain three consequences of leading a sedentary lifestyle on the body's physical function. [3]

Summary

- Health is a state of complete physical, emotional and social well-being.
- Fitness is a body's ability to function efficiently and effectively.
- A healthy, balanced lifestyle includes: healthy diet, regular exercise, healthy body weight, not smoking, limited alcohol intake and minimal stress.
- The benefits of physical activity on the body include:
  - physical: prevents injury, decreases the risk of coronary heart disease and high blood pressure, increased/maintained bone density, prevention of obesity, decreased risk of type 2 diabetes, increased fitness and posture
  - emotional: increased self-esteem and confidence, good stress management and a positive body image
  - social: increased friendship group, feeling of belonging to a group and being socially active.
- A healthy, balanced diet should contain 55 per cent carbohydrates, 15 per cent proteins and no more than 30 per cent fats.
- The components of a balanced diet include:
  - carbohydrates (glucose and glycogen) for energy production
  - proteins for tissue growth and repair and haemoglobin production
  - fats to insulate, cushion and provide an energy store
  - vitamins for blood clotting, eye, tissue and bone health
  - minerals for haemoglobin production, energy production and bone health
  - fibre to aid the large intestine
  - water to help chemical reactions and dissolve and move substances around the body.

Answers

1 Major bones and the function of the skeleton, page 3

1 Tibia and fibula.
2 Radius and ulna.
3 Vertebrae.
4 Cranium.
5 Sternum and ribs.
6 Movement.
7 True.

2 Synovial joints, ligaments, tendons and cartilage, page 5

1 a) Ligament.
  b) Synovial joint.
  c) Hinge joint.
2 Protect the surface of articulating bones, friction-free movement and shock absorption.
3 For example, the Achilles tendon attaches the gastrocnemius to the heel bone.
4 Humerus, radius and ulna.
5 Pelvis and femur.
6 False.
7 True.

3 Movement at hinge and ball and socket joints, page 7

1 a) For example, upward phase of a biceps curl.
  b) For example, execution phase of a kick in football.
  c) For example, outward phase of a star jump.
  d) For example, ballet dancer moving into first position.

2 a) Extension.
  b) Rotation.
  c) Adduction.
  d) Circumduction.
3 True.
4 False.
5 False.

1.1a Exam practice, page 8

1 c) Femur and tibia.
2 a) Humerus and scapula.
3 d) All of the above.
4 (Identification and description required for 1 mark.)

Support/posture: gives shape to the body/holds the body upright/provides a framework.

Protection: keeps internal organs safe/reduces the risk of injury/internal damage (for example, ribs and sternum protect the heart and lungs/cranium protects the brain and so on).

Movement: allows for muscular attachment/creates lever systems/provides leverage.

Blood cell production: bone marrow produces blood cells to replenish/fight infection/transport gases.

Mineral store: bone releases minerals as needed (for example, calcium/iron/potassium).

5 (1 mark for definition and 1 mark for both joints.)

Synovial joint: a freely movable joint where two or more bones articulate.

Shoulder: ball and socket joint.

Knee: hinge joint.

6

Joint	Type of joint	Articulating bones	Movement	Sorting example
Elbow	Hinge	Humerus, radius and ulna	Flexion	For example, upward phase of a biceps curl
Hip	Ball and socket	Pelvis and femur	Extension	Upward phase of a squat

4 Major muscle groups and roles that they play, page 13

1 Biceps and triceps.
2 Gastrocnemius.
3 Flexion.
4 Adduction.
5 Hamstrings.
6 False.
7 True.
8 False.

1.1b Exam practice, page 14

1 **b)** Gluteals.
2 **c)** Latissimus dorsi.
3 **b)** To stabilise one area of the body during movement.
4 (1 mark for definition and 1 mark for appropriate example.)

   Agonist: a muscle which creates movement/the working muscle/a prime mover. For example, the biceps creates/contracts to cause/shortens in length to create flexion of the elbow.
5 Antagonistic pair: the co-ordinating action of an agonist and antagonist muscle/co-ordinated muscular movement/as one muscle creates the movement its pair co-ordinates the action. For example, when lifting a weight in the upward phase the biceps acts as the agonist to create the movement while the triceps co-ordinates the action.

6

Joint	Type of joint	Movement	Agonist	Antagonist
Shoulder	Ball and socket	Abduction	Deltoids	Latissimus dorsi
Knee	Hinge	Extension	Quadriceps	Hamstrings

5 Lever systems, page 16

1 Bone.
2 Joint.
3 Fulcrum – effort – load or load – effort – fulcrum.
4 For example, heading a football where the neck acts as the fulcrum of the first class lever.
5 False.
6 False.
7 A high jumper will take off and jump upwards towards the bar. The lever system at the ball of the foot is an example of a <u>second</u> class lever system. The fulcrum is the joint at the ball of the foot, the effort is the <u>muscular force</u> generated by the gastrocnemius and the load is the <u>weight</u> of the high jumper.

1.1c Exam practice, page 18

1 **d)** Load – fulcrum – effort.
2 **c)** Frontal.
3 **b)** Hip rotation.
4 The ability for a lever system to move a large load with a small effort. It is a second class lever.
5 Third class lever used at the elbow in the upward phase of a biceps curl.

   Third class lever component order: fulcrum – effort – load (or appropriate diagram).

   Lever: radius.

   Fulcrum: elbow joint.

   Effort: muscular force from the biceps.

   Load: weight of the forearm and load in the hand.

6 Planes of movement and axes of rotation, page 17

1 **a)** Sagittal.
   b) Frontal.
   c) Transverse.
2 For example, putting spin on a ball in tennis using rotation of the shoulder.
3 Vertically from top to bottom of the body.
4 False.
5 True.

7 Cardiovascular system, page 21

1 Pulmonary artery from the right ventricle to the lungs. Pulmonary vein from the lungs to the left atrium.
2 Artery.
3 Capillary.

4   The <u>aorta</u> carries oxygenated blood from the left <u>ventricle</u> to the muscles and organs. Oxygen moves through the <u>capillary</u> walls into the tissues and carbon dioxide is collected. The <u>vena cava</u> carries this deoxygenated blood back to the right <u>atrium</u>.

5   True.

6   False.

7   True.

8   Haemoglobin in the red blood cells.

8 Respiratory system, page 24

1   a)   Alveoli.

    b)   Diffusion.

    c)   Breathing rate.

2   VE = *f* × TV or minute ventilation = breathing rate × tidal volume.

3   12–15 breaths per minute.

4   Relax.

5   Nose – trachea – bronchi – bronchioles – alveoli.

9 Aerobic and anaerobic exercise, page 25

1   Aerobic: long duration compared to anaerobic: short duration.

2   Long jump/triple jump/shot-put/discus/100 m sprint and so on.

3   For example, a marathon sustains heart rate and breathing rate over an extended period of around three hours and maintains a moderate pace.

4   Lactic acid production which leads to muscular fatigue and pain.

5   False.

6   True.

7   True.

1.1d Exam practice, page 25

1   d)   Left ventricle.

2   c)   Tidal volume.

3   d)   All of the above.

4   (4 marks for four structures in the correct order.)
    Mouth/nose, trachea, bronchi, bronchioles, alveoli.

5   Cardiac output: The volume of blood ejected from the left ventricle per minute. Calculation: Cardiac output = heart rate × stroke volume or CO = HR × SV.

6   Carry/transport oxygen to the muscles. Carry/transport carbon dioxide to the lungs.

7   Site of gaseous exchange, thin wall/membrane, dense network, large surface area.

8   (Muscles contract to) lift the rib cage up and out.
    Increase the size/volume of the chest/thoracic cavity.
    Decrease the lung/air pressure.

9   (Practical examples must be applied to score marks.)
    (Aerobic) For example, jogging at a steady pace, low intensity and for longer than 20 minutes.
    (Anaerobic) For example, sprinting at maximum/full intensity for 10–20 seconds.
    (Intensity) Aerobic is low/moderate versus anaerobic is high/maximal.
    (Duration) Aerobic is long duration/20 minutes to hours versus anaerobic is short duration/up to 3 minutes.

10 Short-term effects of exercise, page 28

1   False.

2   True.

3   True.

4   The redistribution of blood flow from the organs to the working muscles during exercise.

5   Increased energy production, removal of waste products, increased intensity and duration of performance.

6   Muscular fatigue and pain.

11 Long-term effects of exercise, page 30

1   True.

2   True.

3   False.

4   Hypertrophy of muscles/increased muscular strength/increased fast twitch fibre size/increased resistance to fatigue.
    Increased muscular endurance/increased slow twitch muscle fibre size/increased energy production/train higher intensity for longer duration. ·

5   Heart increases in size/increases in strength which increases SV/decreases HR.

6   Increased strength of respiratory muscles/increased tidal volume during/increased minute ventilation during exercise/increased aerobic capacity.

1.1e Exam practice, page 31

1 **c)** Decreased blood flow to the organs.

2 **b)** Increased bone density.

3 **d)** All of the above.

4 Increased HR/increased SV/increased cardiac output/redistribution of blood flow to the muscles.

5 Increased oxygen delivery/increased nutrient delivery/increased removal of waste products.

6 Increased aerobic capacity/increased ability to use oxygen for energy production which means the marathon runner can perform for longer/the full 27 miles/at a higher intensity/increased pace/resist or delay fatigue.

Increased strength of respiratory muscles/increased force of contraction of diaphragm/intercostals which means increased volume of chest cavity/decreased lung air pressure/inspire more air/increase TV, for example marathon runner can inspire more air to provide oxygen to increase the intensity/increase the pace/last the full 27 miles.

Increased tidal volume/increased minute ventilation which means increased volume of oxygen diffused into bloodstream/removal of waste products/decreased breathing rate as TV increases, for example increased oxygenated blood flow means marathon runner has more potential for aerobic energy production/can run at a higher intensity/increase the pace/last the full 27 miles.

12 Components of fitness, page 33

1 False.

2 True.

3 True.

4 44 ml/kg/min (± 3 ml/kg/min).

5 For example, netball/basketball/volleyball set piece or series of movements that change direction at speed.

6 Handstand requires the gymnast to keep their centre of mass over their base of support to maintain balance.

1.2a Exam practice, page 34

1 **d)** Sit-up test.

2 **c)** A netball goal shooter performing a set piece around the goal circle to get free and receive a ball at speed.

3 **b)** Speed and strength.

4 (1 mark for any appropriate test.) For example, stork stand test.

5 (Definition) The ability to continuously exercise without tiring/VO_2 max/the maximum volume of oxygen taken in and used per minute.

(Appropriate sporting example) For example, marathon/Tour de France cycling/open-water swimming/cross-country skiing.

(Explanation) Long-duration events/low-moderate-intensity events.

6 Multi-stage fitness test: result below average/poor.

Vertical jump test: result above average/good/excellent.

30 m sprint test: result above average/good/excellent.

Sit and reach test: result below average/poor.

(Components for improvement) Aerobic capacity and flexibility.

13 Principles of training, page 36

1 False.

2 True.

3 True.

4 Training should be relevant and appropriate for the individual, sport, muscle fibre type and movement pattern.

5 Low-intensity exercise such as jogging followed by stretching such as quadriceps and hamstring stretches.

6 Reversibility is the maintenance of training to ensure any adaptation to training is not lost. Without using the principle of reversibility there may be a decline in performance.

14 Optimising training, page 39

1 False.

2 False.

3 True.

4 To prepare the body for exercise/prevent injury/increase the temperature of muscles/flexibility/increase the speed of muscle contraction/increase heart rate/gaseous exchange/blood flow/oxygen delivery/carbon dioxide removal.

5 Hopping/bounding/jumping/press-ups with claps.

6 A series of exercises organised into sets of repetitions with an intensity and recovery time specific to the individual.

1.2b Exam practice, page 39

1 **c)** Continuous training.

2 **d)** Jumping on and off boxes.

3 **d)** All of the above.

4 Interval training is periods of exercise followed by periods of <u>rest</u>. It is a common type of training used by <u>aerobic</u> and anaerobic performers, such as games players. Circuit, <u>weight</u>, <u>plyometric</u> and high intensity are all forms of interval training.

5 (First stage) Low-intensity exercise. Activity that gradually decreases temperature and heart and breathing rates, for example jogging.

(Second stage) Stretching. Static stretches that decrease muscle temperature, for example hamstring stretch.

6 Gradual decrease in heart rate/breathing rate/flush muscles with oxygenated blood/remove lactic acid/prevent blood pooling.

Stretches muscles/gradually lowers muscle temperature/realigns muscle fibres/removes waste products/limits delayed onset muscle soreness.

15 Injury prevention, page 42

1 True.

2 True.

3 False.

4 Equipment/floor surface/lack of supervision/poor fitness/lack of technique/lifting equipment.

5 Appropriate examples such as: setting up a trampoline/setting up a table tennis table/lifting weights.

6 Warm-up.

1.2c Exam practice, page 43

1 **b)** Lycra leotard.

2 **d)** All of the above.

3 **c)** Glass on the field.

4 (1 mark for clothing, 1 mark for footwear.)

Correct clothing: allows full range of movement. For example, leotard in gymnastics/has protective padding; BMX biking clothing/can wick away moisture from the skin to prevent overheating; professional football kit material.

Correct footwear: can absorb shock. For example, road running limits wear and tear on knee joint/can increase grip; spikes in athletics give support; arch/ankle/bridge support in tennis shoes.

5 (Definition 1 mark) Something which has the potential to cause harm.

(Example 1 mark) Glass on the pitch/earrings/poor weather conditions/poor fitness, skill or technique/dangerous training practices or environments/inappropriate or damaged clothing or equipment/behaviour of others.

6 High level of fitness/high level of skill/correct technique/correct clothing/correct footwear.

16 Engagement in physical activity and sport in the UK, page 47

1 True.

2 True.

3 True.

4 Sport England/Department for Culture, Media and Sport/Youth Sport Trust/UK Sport/national governing bodies.

5 May provide the opportunity, for example north Wales mountains for climbing and mountain walking. May restrict the opportunity/access, for example, living in the centre of London for white-water rafting. May limit the opportunity for outdoor participation, for example UK climate poor for beach volleyball.

2.1a Exam practice, page 47

1 **c)** 60 minutes of moderate to vigorous physical activity per day.

2 **d)** Rugby Football Union (RFU).

3 **b)** Men participate more than women.

4 Walking/swimming/keep fit or yoga or aerobics or dance exercise/cycling/cue sports or snooker or pool or billiards.

5 Age/gender/ethnicity or religion or culture/family/education/time or work commitments/cost or disposable income/disability/opportunity or access/environment or climate/media coverage/role models.

6 (1 mark for an appropriate strategy and 1 mark for description.)

This Girl Can/girls-only classes/girls-only hour and so on.

Strategy to raise the confidence/esteem/image of women in sport to encourage participation/promote opportunities/role models/choices to participate.

17 Commercialisation of sport, page 50

1 True.
2 False.
3 False.
4 Post-match discussion in chat groups, for example WhatsApp, photos at sports matches on Facebook, Instagram and so on.
5 Increases participation/generates funding/makes sport more entertaining/makes game fairer/24-hour worldwide coverage/increases national pride/promotes minority sports/promotes good role models and breaks stereotypes/creates sports stars on and off field.
6 Bad image for sport. For example, alcohol or fast food/pressure of sponsor demands/unequal sponsorship – only for a few top sports or teams/not secure funding or easily lost.

2.1b Exam practice, page 50

1 **b)** The words 'Standard Chartered' on Liverpool's football kit.
2 **d)** The funding of sport: individuals, teams or kits to make a profit.
3 **d)** All of the above.
4 The relationship between and interdependence of the media, sport and sponsorship.
5 (1 mark description and 1 mark appropriate example.)

Increased funding/money to sport which can improve facilities/standards/coaching/equipment/pays for competitions or events and so on.

Allows full-time training/to turn professional/sporting career.

Gives financial security.

Any appropriate example. For example, the London Virgin Marathon funded by Virgin Money.
6 (Do not award mark if no sporting example given.)

Too much focus on sport: people would rather watch than participate. For example, major football competition: more time spent in pub/at home than out participating/being active.

Pay per view limits access: those who cannot afford subscriptions are limited to what and when they can watch. For example, Premiership football.

Poor role models highlighted. For example, swearing or violence or arguing with the referee.

Damaging press coverage: intrusion into players' personal lives/pre-match hype/negativity towards opponents. For example, David Beckham affair/England versus Germany football matches.

Minority sports limited coverage. For example, table tennis/high-board diving only shown during Olympics.

Controls or changes sport. For example, excessive number of cameras or lights/changed start times.

18 Ethical and socio-cultural issues in physical activity and sport, page 54

1 False.
2 True.
3 False.
4 Illegal drug use.
5 An appropriate example of anger/frustration/intensity of a game/abuse or provocation/lack of discipline or punishments/nature of the game/equipment.
6 To improve physical function (for example build muscle/lose weight/mask pain)/train harder/improve psychological function (for example steady nerves/increase motivation/alertness/aggression)/to win at all costs/belief others are doing it/belief won't get caught.

2.1c Exam practice, page 54

1 **c)** Delaying play by changing rackets unnecessarily in tennis.
2 **a)** Weightlifters.
3 **d)** All of the above
4 If a player is provoked or abused. For example, crowd chanting abuse from the stands in rugby/a bad tackle from an opponent in football/verbal abuse or sledging in cricket.
5 Lowers status of sport/creates bad name for the sport/lowers respect for the sport/bad publicity.

Costs money to test/investigate/accuse/convict an athlete of drug taking.

Clean athletes/new records questioned.
6 Gamesmanship is unethical bending of the rules/not breaking the rules to gain an unfair advantage/not illegal compared to deviance.

Deviance is cheating/breaking of rules of sport/often illegal.

A tennis player breaking their opponent's serve to put a new grip on their racket, compared to a tennis player taking anabolic steroids to increase power.

19 Characteristics of skilful movement and skill classification, page 56

1 False.
2 True.
3 False.
4 Close to the complex end of the difficulty continuum/close to the open end of the environmental continuum.
5 For example, a gymnastic leap that looks pleasing to the eye.

20 Goal setting, page 57

1 False.
2 False.
3 True.
4 Specific/Measurable/Achievable/Recorded/ Timed.
5 Specific/realistic/achievable/recorded goals keep a performer on track/motivate/give drive/can see progress/achieve success.

21 Mental preparation, page 58

1 True.
2 True.
3 False.
4 Imagery/mental rehearsal/selective attention/ positive thinking.
5 For example, a high-board diver goes through the dive in their head to form a mental image of the dive about to be performed.

22 Types of guidance and feedback, page 60

1 True.
2 True.
3 False.
4 Positive feedback gives information about successful outcomes whereas negative feedback gives information about unsuccessful outcomes.
5 For example, using a harness to learn a somersault in gymnastics/trampolining/high-board diving to increase safety/reduce fear/raise confidence/give a kinaesthetic feel.

2.2 Exam practice, page 60

1 a) A tennis player performing a serve and immediately continuing to volley at the net.
2 c) A hockey pass.
3 d) Motor skill.
4 c) Manual guidance.
5 c) Negative.
6 (Closed skill) A motor skill unaffected by environmental conditions, for example a tennis/ badminton/table tennis serve.

 (Complex skill) A motor skill which requires a performer to make many judgements/decisions, for example a pass in hockey.
7 Difficulty continuum of simple to complex skills.

 Complex skills require the performer to make many judgements/decisions, for example a netball interception.

 Simple skills require the performer to make few judgements/decisions, for example a sprint start in athletics.
8 (1 mark) Adhere to exercise/motivate performers or improve/optimise performance.

 (3 marks from) Specific: goals clear/focused, for example weight loss exercise programme goal of losing 2 cm from waist circumference after six weeks of aerobic exercise.

 Measurable: goals assessed to know how well a performer has done, for example measure how many times a gymnast completes a cartwheel with perfect technique.

 Achievable: goals realistic and within the performer's capability, for example if a netball team scored 12 goals in the first quarter, a goal of 13 in the second quarter.

 Recorded: measurements/progress logged to track progress/adapt training programmes or future goals, for example a weightlifter records the number of sets, reps and weight lifted each session to ensure there is progress.

 Timed: short-term goals are more achievable/ break down goals into realistic time periods, for example a one-week goal for training to improve the sprint-start technique.
9 A performer concentrates on relevant information/cues or a performer ignores distractions/irrelevant cues. For example, a footballer focuses on team mates, marker and the goal when playing a ball upfield.
10 (1 mark for appropriate practical example, 1 mark for an advantage and 1 mark for a disadvantage.)

 A tennis coach/instructor giving a demonstration/ video/chart/illustration of the perfect serving technique.

(Advantage) Good for beginners/easy to remember/technical model to copy/quick/effective/builds a mental picture.

(Disadvantage) Hard to get a feel for the skill/wrong outcome if demonstration is incorrect/too complicated/overloads information.

11 (An attempt at comparative language for 2 marks.)

Knowledge of performance is feedback about the movement; knowledge of results is feedback about the end result.

Knowledge of performance can come from the feel of the movement/intrinsic/kinaesthetic feedback; knowledge of results usually comes from seeing their performance/coach/instructor.

12 Manual guidance physically supports the performer whereas mechanical guidance uses equipment to support the performer.

They reduce fear in dangerous situations, for example a supportive hand under the stomach or float used for a novice swimmer.

Increase safety, for example physical support or a harness used to help a full rotation in gymnastics.

Raise confidence, for example a spotter or hydraulic machine gives added support and reassurance to a weightlifter.

23 Health, fitness and well-being, page 64

1 True.
2 False.
3 True.
4 Prevents injury/decreases the risk of coronary heath disease (CHD)/decreases the risk of high blood pressure/increases or maintains bone density/prevents obesity/limits type 2 diabetes/increases fitness/maintains good posture.
5 Decreased self-esteem or confidence/poor management of stress/negative body image.
6 Poor body image/lack of opportunities for involvement/lack of ways to release stress/lack of social interaction/isolation/loneliness.

24 Diet and nutrition, page 65

1 False.
2 True.
3 True.
4 Eating a wide variety of food, including five portions of fruit and vegetables per day/55 per cent carbohydrates, 15 per cent proteins and no more than 30 per cent fats.

5 Large constituent of blood/allows chemical reactions/dissolves or moves substances around the body.
6 Increase glycogen levels/produce energy for longer/produce more energy/delay fatigue/perform or train for longer.

2.3 Exam practice, page 66

1 **d)** Absorbing stress.
2 **c)** Positive body image.
3 **b)** 55 per cent carbohydrates, 15 per cent protein and no more than 30 per cent fats.
4 (Sporting example must be used to gain mark.)

Increased friendship group. For example, netball opportunity to meet new people/training/football matches/share experiences/basketball work cooperatively with team mates/set pieces.

Belonging to a group. For example, feel part of a team/netball squad lists or jumpers.

Socially active. For example, opportunities for social gatherings/football awards/occasions and gatherings/basketball matches or end of league celebrations.

5 (1 mark carbohydrates, 1 mark proteins. Sporting example must be used to gain marks.)

Carbohydrates are essential for energy production. For example, carbohydrates are main fuel for energy/muscle movement in footballers.

Proteins are essential for tissue growth/repair/haemoglobin production. For example, proteins help to repair muscle/tendon/tissues after heavy weight training.

6 Increased risk of injury *due to* poor joint flexibility/strength/stability.

Increased risk of coronary heart disease/high blood pressure *due to* reduced circulation/blood flow/high cholesterol levels/blood fats/low removal or usage of fat.

Low bone density *due to* lack of bone growth or renewal/lack of stress placed on bone/lack of calcium deposits.

Leads to obesity/type 2 diabetes *due to* low energy levels/high stores of body fat/high circulating levels of blood sugars.

Poor fitness and posture *due to* low energy levels/weakness/lethargy/out of breath easily/early onset of fatigue/weak core muscles.